MY JOURNEY OUT OF THE BOTTLE

Four Rehabs and a Recovery

JANE MUSGRAVE

Published by: Miss Jane's Diary

Brisbane, QLD, AUS

Paperback ISBN: 978-1-7642967-0-0
Ebook ISBN: 978-1-7642967-1-7

Copyright © 2025 by Jane Musgrave
All rights reserved, including the right of reproduction in whole or in part of any form.

Printed in the Australia

Jane loves hearing from readers. You can reach her at missjane1366@gmail.com

Dedication

To my amazing family and friends,
thank you for not giving up on me.

Table of Contents

Part One. The First Rehab

Chapter One. Rock Bottom 1

Chapter Two. The Early Years of my Drinking Career 11

Chapter Three. The Marriage, the Drinking,
the Gambling and The Abuse 15

Chapter Four. Escape from the Ex –
How I Ended up in my First Rehab 23

Chapter Five. Life After the First Rehab – Sobriety Take One 31

Chapter Six. The Romance Scam 37

Chapter Seven. My First Relapse 45

Chapter Eight. My Three Year Bender 55

Chapter Nine. Cheeky Monkey 63

Chapter Ten. Lets Get Dry 71

Part Two. The Second Rehab

Chapter Eleven. Déjà vu 79

Chapter Twelve. Life After the Second Rehab – Sobriety Take Two 85

Chapter Thirteen. Drink Like There is no Tomorrow 91

Part Three. The Third Rehab

Chapter Fourteen. The Retreat 99

Chapter Fifteen. The Break Through 107

Chapter Sixteen. Life After the Third Rehab – Sobriety Take Three . . . 115

Chapter Seventeen. Will I Ever learn? 123

Chapter Eighteen. I Become a Race Car Driver at Age Fifty Six! 131

Chapter Ninteen. The Brink of Self Destruction 141

Part Four. The Fourth Rehab

Chapter Twenty. The Turning Point.............................. 149
Chapter Twenty One. The Rules................................. 157
Chapter Twenty Two. My Breaking Point 165
Chapter Twenty Three. The All Important Epiphany 171
Chapter Twenty Four. The Funny Farm........................ 179

The Recovery

Chapter Twenty Five. Life After the Fourth Rehab –
Sobriety Take Four.. 185
Chapter Twenty Six. Racing and Rebuilding 191
Chapter Twenty Seven. Gypsy Jane 197
Chapter Twenty Eight. Finding my Gift......................... 207
Today.. 217

PART ONE

The First Rehab

CHAPTER ONE

Rock Bottom

I felt like a failure, scraping the bottom of the barrel. Me, Jane, going to rehab—how did my life come to this?

The shame welled inside me as my Mum drove me to the rehab centre, It is located within a private hospital in Brisbane. The redbrick building came into view, and I knew my life would change, but it needed to. I could barely look at my mother. A mix of emotions swelling inside of me. I felt like a loser, a no-good drunk from an old-fashioned movie sprawled in the gutter, and I hated myself.

The red Honda hatchback came to a slow stop. A heavy sigh slipped out, not knowing what to say. Mum always knew best, she was always there to pick up the pieces. She took me by the arm and we walked into the building. Inside, the fluorescent lights stabbed at my already aching eyes, still hungover from the night before, I had drowned myself with last drinks, my head pounding, just like any other normal day really. I could smell the alcohol coming out of my pores, but my mother ignored it.

The lady at the reception desk was clicking her pen. Each time it snapped my head throbbed even more.

What's your name Love?.

"Jane Musgrave," my mother answered for me, as I tried to avoid eye contact with everyone.

The administrator looked at me, with slight empathy. I am sure she had seen a thousand Jane's before, but this moment was the most shameful in my life. She handed me some papers to sign. Before today, I would have been sitting here so confidently, the person in charge, I was a functioning alcoholic. No one knew, not my coworkers, not my social circle, no one.

My admission to the clinic was now complete. Relief came with the knowledge my Health Insurance will cover the staggering $14,000 cost. The nurse clipped the plastic identification tag on my arm, pointed to the elevator and told me to go up to the third floor and report to the nurses' station. I stood up, grabbed my suitcase, the reality hitting me like a medicine ball being thrown at my chest. It was heartbreaking, I hugged my Mum and said goodbye, trying not to cry. She held a stiff upper lip, telling me everything would be okay.

Coming out of the elevator on the rehab floor was daunting, I was by myself, I felt like I had let everyone I loved down, I was the worst person in the world. I found the nurses' station and handed over my paperwork. There were two female nurses' and a male nurse, they introduced themselves and I immediately felt safe. They were so kind and caring and I knew they had my best interests at heart.

One of the nurses' guided me to a chair next to a trolley with a blood pressure monitor, and other leads and devices stacked on it. She cusped the band around my arm. The plastic felt cool but within seconds a layer of condensation appeared. The machine beeped, which wasn't helping my hangover. Also, the pinch of the oxygen monitor on my finger annoyed me.

The nurse clucked her tongue. "That's not good."

I stared at her vaguely.

"Your blood pressure, it's alarmingly high, I'm happy you made it to us." She gave me a reassuring smile.

"I'm scared," I admitted. Something that was hard for me to even admit to myself.

She placed a reassuring arm around my shoulder. "How long have you been drinking? How bad is it?"

"I have been drinking seven days a week, fifty-two weeks of the year for thirty years. You tell me." My voice had a bitter edge on it.

"It is a good thing you are here. If you had stopped drinking cold turkey, your brain and body could have had a violent reaction… there can be seizures… psychosis… anyway it is good you are here. Let's get you some Diazepam for the detox it will help. I promise."

She handed me a small white paper cup with pills that I would become all too familiar with two x 5mg (milligrams), I will be required to have 10mg four times per day to start.

I put the cup to my lips and swallowed the pills, chased by a glass of water. Both things that my body desperately needed.

The nurse smiled kindly at me and led me by the arm to my room. By the time we reached the door I had a lovely floating sensation coursing through my body.

The nurse smiled wider as she saw my body relax. "It will help ease you off of the alcohol as painlessly as possible." The nurse opened the door. "What do you think?"

The room is a sickly beige colour and set up as a standard hospital room, a bed, a shared bathroom and toilet connected with the next room, a set of drawers, a table, chair and a window. No television, nothing fancy at all. It's very clinical, my outer calmness crumbles and I burst into tears. "It's not very nice, but it is all I deserve, I am just devastated to be here". "I know, but look at the view of this lovely tree." She walked me to the window. A huge tree fills the entire window space.

It's lunchtime. The nurse escorts me to the dining room and explains how meals work on weekdays versus weekends. Today is Friday, and the other patients are already eating. I scan the room, freeze, and feel the humiliation flare. Sensing my distress, the nurse steers me to the sandwich bar and suggests I take something back to my room. I nod, tears spilling again.

My room feels even gloomier now, so I wander the corridors in search of the television room. I finally settle into a single recliner and lose myself in *The Bold and the Beautiful*, pure mind-numbing distraction.

Not long after, one of the nurses' finds me, brightly telling me it's time for observations (obs) and more medication (meds). This, I'm happy for, I want that relaxing feeling to keep my nerves calm. After I take the two little pills in the white paper cup, the nurse has me hold my hands out to see if I have the shakes. I don't, which is a good sign, no withdrawal symptoms.

I opt to have dinner in my room, not ready to be social with others yet. I'm still so disgusted with myself for being here. As I eat the hospital-style meal, I pray for this day to end so I can sleep and forget everything for a while.

Afterward came a shower, the slow routine of preparing for bed, then a stop at the nurses' station for nighttime obs, meds, and yet another round of hand-shake tests. Back in the room, the hospital bed offered little comfort: starchy sheets, a flat pillow, a plastic mattress that squeaked with every movement. Rest seemed unlikely, the night stretching out ahead with little promise of peace.

Waking restless in the early hours, I get out of the squeaky bed and head to the nurses' station for more meds. Back into bed for more broken sleep.

Saturday dawns, and nothing has changed, the same drab room, and I still feel miserable. More obs and meds start the day, then I venture into the dining room for breakfast, trying to give a slight smile to the others there. After a quick meal of cereal and toast, I scurry away to find a spot in the sun to read a book.

One of the nurses' finds me, she needs to take my blood. A full blood work up is required to see what thirty years of alcohol consumption has done to my body. A small blessing in my life is the fact I drink an insane amount of water, at least three litres per day, always.

I go to the television room, find a couple of others, introduce myself, and we watch a few of hours of TV. Back in my depressing room, I call my Mum to let her know how I'm coping, how much I hate it, but that I know I have to do this if there's any chance of getting off alcohol. My emotions overwhelm me again, and I'm crying, just hating my life.

Dinner time rolls around, and I eat in the dining room with some of the other patients. The room is set up like a self-serve canteen, a line of bain-maries with hot food, bread and butter at the end, and a little fridge with desserts. The food is okay; at this stage, I don't care what it tastes like, as I'm still beating myself up for being here. On the other hand, I'm very interested in the dessert selection, sugar and sweets are becoming my new best friend!

A few of us watch another TV show, then it's time for bed. More obs, more meds, my hands not shaking, and I'm doing well, so they cut the medication dose to start weaning me off the Diazepam. I'm now alcohol-free, the last thing I need is to become dependent on a different substance.

It's Saturday night, and I'm looking forward to tomorrow, Sunday and Mother's Day. My son, his girlfriend, and my Mum are coming to visit me. I feel devastated to be here on this special day; I cry myself to sleep.

They arrive around 10:00 a.m. on Mother's Day. The joy of seeing them is overwhelming. I'm so happy but feel so guilty about being here, like I'm in jail. On the other hand, knowing they support me through this makes everything worthwhile.

We walk to the cafe next door to the hospital for coffee, milkshakes and cake. I tell them of my experience so far, trying not to cry. The visit ends all too soon. We walk back to the hospital, say our goodbyes, and they assure me this is for the best, I will come out a new person.

Monday arrives, at the nurses' station, I'm given an even lower dose of medication 5mg to be taken four times today. Then I'm called to my room where the doctor I was referred to is waiting. This is our first meeting, and we immediately form a good rapport. He sets my mind at ease, telling me it's okay and normal to feel as I do; he'd be worried if I didn't feel these emotions.

I tell him how hard it is to let go of my past, the hold my ex-husband still has on me. He shares a fantastic analogy. It is referring to Homer Simpson with his hand stuck in a beer vending machine. No one can get it unstuck, not the Fire Department, Ambulance, or Council. Then Moe, the bartender, says to Homer, "Let go of the can," and his hand comes free. It's just like letting go of the past. I remember that every time I struggle to let something go.

After the doctor's visit, I'm starting to feel better about being here. I say to myself, "I don't ever want to end up here again!"

I can now start participating in the classes. A two-week schedule is handed to me, and it needs to be stamped after every lesson to prove my attendance. The classes are set in rooms with desks, chairs, and a whiteboard, just like being back at school. At 48, I find myself back in a classroom, and I can't help but laugh. They say you're never too old to learn.

The classes are run by therapists, each focusing on different aspects of what they're teaching us. We receive training manuals to follow and make notes in, our bible for the next two weeks and for when we return home. The first day's classes focus on devaluing alcohol and ending the love affair with it. I hear the best advice: "Start to get into a routine." I'll discuss the importance of this in a later chapter.

Art therapy classes quickly became my favourite. As a creative person, I love hands-on learning. The task was to go through magazines and cut out pictures of what our life looked like while drinking out of control, then cut out pictures of what we want our life to look like going forward. We stuck them all onto two separate sheets of coloured paper, these we can look back at when back out in the real world, to motivate us, to keep working towards sobriety. These classes relax me, and I continue to use this therapy to this day.

On Monday afternoon, I meet with a psychologist and share my story. She tells me I've been a victim of domestic violence, abuse, and control since meeting my ex-husband. I read from my journal, where I am blaming myself for the situation, thinking that earlier rehab might have given my son a better life or strengthened me to leave. She shuts me down immediately, telling me to stop berating myself. I didn't ask to be treated this way, and now I must look after myself to care for others.

I get to know the other patients; we're all here for the same reason and support each other. For safety reasons, we don't share last names, phone numbers, or social media details. I'm fully on board with this, I will have my own problems when I leave and don't want any other distractions.

The next morning, the doctor stops by my room for his daily visit, this will happen every weekday between 7.00 and 8.00am. He has the results for my blood tests, I hold my breath and brace for the bad news. I have an enlarged fatty liver, no surprise there, and the rest of my health is very good. I am pleasantly surprised and give thanks to my love of drinking water. With me it was either water or wine, water all day, wine all night!!

The classes continue and I am fully detoxed. I note an interesting topic in my journal: the Grief Process. *We must let go of alcohol and grieve for it, like a death.* I decided to do this for both alcohol and my ex-husband. "Grieve for both, then move on." *Emotions must be dealt with, listen to whispers before they become screams*, great advice.

The next weekend, visitors are allowed, and Mum comes to see me. We walk through the Roma Street Parklands and into the city for lunch. It's a beautiful spring day with a deep blue sky, and the flowers are in full bloom, their perfume permeating the air. Mum sees the change in me, and she's happy and proud. I feel different too, accepting I'm an alcoholic but knowing I can fix it by staying strong and not drinking. Simple.

The second week is pretty much a repeat of the first, sleep, eat, lessons, learn, but we have a special visitor one evening. A gentleman from an Alcoholics Anonymous (AA) group comes in to talk to us about meetings. He's been sober for 12 years, an impressive achievement. But I dismiss his message, thinking AA is religious and not wanting to be preached to about God. I tune out, say no thank you, and walk away... Big mistake, Jane!

After a total of 14 days, I've completed the program and am free to go. The clinic offers day rehab, but I need to return to Central Queensland for work, so I opt for weekly phone calls to check on my progress.

On Friday afternoon, walking out of that clinic, I feel like a new person, determined never to drink again. I know it will be a challenge, but I'm resolved never to feel as I did when I first walked through those doors. Little did I know, this would not be the case, and oh boy, did I fall off the wagon!

My first time in rehab. The following is an exact extract from the journal I started upon entering rehab; it is raw and brutally honest.

09th May 2014 – Admission Day. All good so far, my observations have been taken, and I am shown to my room by the nurse, who explains the rules. I sit in the room until the nurse comes and takes me to the dining room for lunch and explains the weekday procedures. I tear up and lose it, so we go back to my room, and the nurse tells me it's all ok. It's so overwhelming, and I have lunch in my room. After a good cry and lots more explanations, I get a tour of the facility and fill out more forms, then there are more tears.

I am HUMILIATED to be here, I HATE the room, so I go and find a TV to watch B&B. I have more observations (obs) taken and have some medication, then I opt for dinner in my room. I try to get the TV on my phone but just waste my data. More obs and more medication and I go to sleep at 9.30. I wake up restless at 2.30am and get some more medication. I then wake up at 6.45am, the nurse comes in at 7.30 and I go for obs and medication. I am feeling anxious and end up in tears again. I head off for breakfast and settle down to some reading. More doctors followed by morning tea and I am still trying to cope that I am in here and I have more medication. I start feeling a bit better and I decide I DO NOT EVER WANT TO END UP HERE EVER AGAIN.

I hope to watch TV later, and I suggest to the nurse that I might attend the BBQ tomorrow. I have no cravings yet, just anxiety. I watch TV and talk to Mum on the phone. I am still crying, and I still blame my ex-husband for this, why should he be happy and cut me off when I needed his help, well that's going to change!!! More obs and medication, then dinner and go to watch a show with some other people in there until 9.30pm then obs, medication, shower and bed. I am looking forward to a visit tomorrow from my son. It is Mother's Day tomorrow and I am in here.

How did I get here…?

CHAPTER TWO

The Early Years of my Drinking Career

I was a rebellious teenager, troubled upbringing, parents divorced, both with new partners and I inherited extra siblings, and it is NOT like the Brady Bunch, let's just add alcohol to the mix and see what happens.

At fifteen, I tasted alcohol for the first time, Bundaberg rum, to be specific. The taste wasn't pleasant, but the warmth as it slid down my throat, followed by a buzzy sensation, was thrilling. By the end of that glass, my lips and cheeks were numb, and I was captivated by that feeling.

Alcohol became my confidence booster. As a relatively shy teenager, it transformed me into someone outgoing, eager to talk and dance. My first drunken escapade was with rum, which left me awfully sick. I was at a friend's sleepover, drinking away from my dad's watchful eye. As we left the party, my friends warned I needed to sober up or throw up before heading back to her place.

They laid me on a trampoline, jumping around to induce nausea, but it only made me flop around like a rag doll. Back at her house, still drunk, I went to bed, a mistake. The room spun, my stomach churned, and I dashed to the toilet, colliding with her dad. I wasn't the favourite guest for a week after that.

That experience turned me off rum but my intrigue with alcohol only grew. I wanted more of this magical liquid that took all my worries away. It made me feel popular, and banished my shyness. I craved more.

On my 16th birthday, I landed a job as a receptionist at an electrical retail company, starting the following Monday. I loved the job and the camaraderie with the staff. Late-night shopping was just emerging, and Saturdays ended at noon. I joined the staff after work for drinks, trying Scotch for the first time. The taste didn't win me over, but the feeling did. Saturdays became a regular drinking affair, I was hooked.

With my own income, I started clubbing with my high school friend, who I fondly nicknamed Stix, who remains very dear to me. We'd bus into town with $10.20 each, twenty cents for the fare, $5 for a bottle each of Ben Ean Moselle, and the rest for a taxi home. Our nights were filled with drinking and dancing from Wednesday to Saturday, frequenting venues like the Court Jester in Brisbane City, the Mansfield Tavern for live bands and the Calamvale Tavern for Friday night shenanigans. Those nights were a blur of fun and familiarity, surrounded by people from our rough but beloved neighborhood, Acacia Ridge.

This routine continued for years: work, drink, party, repeat. The hangovers continued to get worse too, some days getting out of bed was impossible and my work was suffering. The venues changed, but the drinking persisted. It never occurred to me then that alcohol dependency might be an issue. I was simply having a blast.

At 22, living with my best friend (who is still my bestie and biggest supporter). I stumbled upon an article on alcohol consumption. It claimed preferring drinks over meals indicated alcoholism. I thought, "That's me!" wine and cheese often sufficed for dinner. This was the first time I recognized I might have a problem. I attempted to cut back, skipping alcohol on Mondays and Tuesdays. I had now included Sundays on my social calendar, the afternoon session at Fisherman's Wharf on the Gold Coast.

In July 1990 at the age 24, I joined the Royal Australian Air Force (RAAF), driven by a love for flying and aircraft. I headed to Adelaide for basic training, facing three months with limited alcohol, a daunting prospect. Discipline was another hurdle, as I wasn't one to follow orders.

Skeptics doubted I'd complete the training, given its physical demands and my aversion to exercise. Running 2.5 kilometers in 15 minutes seemed miraculous, this was a requirement to graduate!! On the 18th July, the Queensland contingent of recruits arrived at the training base in Elizabeth on the outskirts of Adelaide, settling into a cold, clinical dormitory. Each room housed four, with basic amenities and a bar heater for warmth.

We were taught to make beds to military standards, with hospital corners tight enough to bounce a coin. The dorm's upkeep was our responsibility, from daily cleaning of the ablutions to polishing the lino floors twice a week. The next three months became a mentally and physically challenging yet enjoyable experience. I managed with minimal alcohol, a personal triumph, though when permitted, I indulged with mixed outcomes.

The base "Boozer" offered cheap drinks, pool, and jukebox tunes on weekends. Missteps during the week meant a ban, so I stayed on my best behavior. After graduating from basic training, we all headed to Wagga Wagga, NSW, for role-specific training, mine was as a Clerk Supply. Rules were relaxed, allowing nightly visits to the Boozer. I limited my partying to Thursdays through Saturdays, also venturing into town to enjoy Wagga's vibrant nightlife.

These nights, filled with live acts and clubs, came with consequences, bad hangovers, poor decisions, even fainting on parade. Upon completing training, I received my posting: the Air Force Base in Richmond, west of Sydney, NSW. It was late December and we all headed home to spend Christmas with families. January 1991 arrived, I packed up my sports car and drove to Richmond, my new home for the next five years.

Life on base was a dream, with work nearby, meals at the mess, a cinema, and a Boozer. Every second Thursday, pay day, a disco on base, meaning more drinks and dancing. The defence force's drinking culture was robust, encouraging my blossoming alcoholism. The Boozer was the go-to spot, life was great, I was in my element.

That year, life was set to change, shaping who I am today, for better or worse…

CHAPTER THREE

The Marriage, the Drinking, the Gambling and The Abuse

Life on base felt like a dream, a crisp routine wrapped in the comfort of camaraderie and order. I had no idea how quickly that world would tilt. In October 1991 a mutual friend introduced me to a man who, without warning, would unravel everything. He was in town, training to become a dog handler with the New South Wales Department of Corrections. At first glance, he barely registered. But he was persistent, always around, always charming in a way that slowly slipped under my skin.

We shared a love for a good drink, having the easy kind of connection that seems harmless at first. But beneath his easy grin lay something darker, an obsession with poker machines. I'd grown up in Queensland, where those machines were outlawed, and gambling was as foreign to me as snow. Still, as our relationship deepened, I found myself by his side in smoky clubs, where flashing lights and clinking coins became our backdrop. I learned my limits quickly, especially after losing more money than I care to admit. He never did. Losses only fueled him, he chased them with a desperation I didn't yet recognize as addiction.

By mid-1992, we were living together, and by October, engaged. I told myself love was enough, that I could help him through his compulsions, that I could fix it. But nights out became a ritual: I'd be sipping a drink while he fed the machines like they held the answers to all his problems. We had little in common beyond our vices. I turned a blind eye to the cash he blew; he overlooked how much I drank. We were enabling each other in the worst possible ways.

Even when the warning signs screamed, I clung to hope. But it only got worse. Now he was controlling me. He didn't like me talking to other men, and didn't trust me to go out alone. He'd insist I sit next to him at the poker machines, as if proximity alone could prove my loyalty. If I so much as smiled at someone or stayed for a drink after work, accusations would fly. And they stung, I was loyal. I was just being my happy cheery self.

Still, I stayed. I believed in perseverance, in commitment. In October 1993, we married in my hometown of Brisbane. It was a beautiful ceremony, full of laughter and love. Our honeymoon was a modest road trip back to Sydney, lined with photo ops and roadside cafés. But the illusion shattered quickly. One night, he dumped our entire honeymoon budget, $1,000, into a poker machine. Just like that, it was gone. I was stunned, sickened, and yet, I stayed,

The years blurred into a pattern of drinking, hangovers, gambling, and quiet devastation. In 1995, a car accident, resulting in ruptured discs in my lower back, cut short my military career. I was medically discharged from the Air Force, and we moved to Brisbane. I started working in my parents' audio-visual shop as their Office Manager, while he stayed on with Corrections. We rented a house, and the cycle resumed. Now, poker machines were legal in Queensland. He was in his element again, and I was drowning.

In 1996, we bought our first small home. It should have been a turning point. Instead, it marked a new phase of decline. With a mortgage looming, I tried to tighten the purse strings. That's when the emotional abuse began in earnest. His words turned sharp, cutting deeper than any argument. He chipped away at my confidence until I started to believe the worst about myself. I withdrew, lost touch with friends. He monitored everything—where I went, who I spoke to. The walls of that house were solid brick, but I felt like I was living in a cage and my drinking only increased.

After years of trying to add to our family, I finally became pregnant, our baby due in August 1997. It was a joyful time. I wasn't drinking, and he, for a while, cut back on his own drinking to support me. The day our son was born remains the happiest of my life. But, just hours after his birth, my husband left the hospital to celebrate, at the pub. He returned later with a teddy bear for our boy, but no flowers for me. It stung, but I was too elated with our healthy son to dwell on it.

Two months later, reality crashed in. I was diagnosed with postnatal depression. It was my beautiful, kind neighbor who opened the door to that realization. She left a pamphlet about this very thing on her kitchen bench while I was visiting. I picked it up, scanned the checklist, and by the end, my hands were trembling. Every symptom stared back at me like a mirror. "That's me," I whispered.

I sought help. My doctor prescribed medication to rebalance the storm inside my head. Now I was grappling with a fractured marriage, escalating depression, and a deepening reliance on alcohol to numb the pain. Still I was striving to be the best mother I could. My husband offered little support, often at work or the pub, yet criticized my efforts as a wife and mother.

April 1998. My father passed away. Only six months earlier, doctors had spoken the words *pancreatic cancer*—a diagnosis that feels like a death sentence even before it is explained. The disease is merciless, fast, and then, too soon, on Easter Thursday, he was called back to heaven.

He was only fifty-eight.

The loss shattered me. Grief presses into my chest like a weight I can't lift. Yet, in the midst of sorrow, I cling to one gift: my father had met his grandson. For eight precious months, I watched him cradle that small, wriggling body, hear his laughter soften in a way I hadn't heard before, and saw a light in his eyes that illness couldn't dim.

A few years down the line, we had sold our first house, and bought a bigger house closer to my husband's work. Then he decided he preferred to live in the area we were previously, so we sold our second home and found ourselves renting, searching for the next place to call ours. By now, I reached a breaking point. The relentless cycle of gambling, financial stress, and emotional erosion finally cracked something in me. While we were not locked into a mortgage I decided it was the right time to tell him I couldn't go on like this. I laid it bare, either things changed, or I was done.

He begged me to stay. Promised less gambling. Promised change. I wanted to believe him. I needed to. So I stayed, and soon we bought our third house, clinging to the hope that new walls might somehow shelter a new beginning.

But the patterns repeated. The gambling. The drinking. The empty promises. I gave up trying to fight it and joined in. "If you can't beat them, join them," I thought, and my drinking escalated again, dulling the edges of a life I no longer recognized.

Two and a half years later, we sold again and headed north, chasing the illusion of a fresh start. Cairns greeted us with sun-drenched skies and a breathtaking view, our new home perched above the ocean, islands dotting the horizon like scattered jewels. It was paradise on the surface. But the heat was stifling, the humidity relentless. And inside our beautiful home, the same storms raged.

My husband's job was situated on the Atherton Tablelands, an hour's drive inland from Cairns, winding up the Kuranda Range through rainforest and over the plains towards the Great Dividing Range. The commute for him and the relentless humidity wore us down, seeping into our tempers and our routines. After just nine months, we gave up our ocean view and sold the house, moving closer to his work in search of something easier.

What we found felt like a kind of peace. Our new home sat on two and a half acres at the base of the majestic Range, surrounded by waterfalls and forest. It was quiet in a way that city life never allowed. Here, we found a semblance of happiness. Country living suited us, with fewer pubs and clubs to tempt us.

We bought a small fishing boat, nothing fancy, spent days on Lake Tinaroo, fishing and setting pots for red claw lobsters. Though the gambling lessened, our drinking remained excessive.

After three good years, we made the difficult decision to leave. My stepfather's health was deteriorating, bone cancer was stealing him away inch by inch. I needed to be closer to my mother, to help carry the weight she could no longer shoulder alone. My husband, ever in love with the open land and its stillness, agreed. He understood the pull of family, even if it meant letting go of the place where we had finally begun to feel whole.

Back in Brisbane, we bought another beautiful house, a dream house. Four bedrooms, two bathrooms, two living areas, a formal dining room and a resort style inground pool, but cracks in our relationship widened. My husband resented the move, and the mental abuse resurfaced. I knew I needed to leave, but drinking clouded my resolve. Seeking help to cut down, I turned to my doctor for guidance on quitting, there was mention of me thinking about going to a rehab, "no fucking way" I said, I'm not that bad. Therapy and medication offered brief relief, but his behavior wore me down. I gave up trying to quit drinking; it numbed the pain of living with him.

By 2009, after 16 years of marriage, his abuse reached a tipping point. I declared I couldn't endure it any longer, asked for a divorce, and told him to leave. He left, but returned the next day, full of apologies, promises and also threats to take his life if I didn't take him back. I, softened by alcohol and sympathy, let him back in, yet I knew I had to plan my escape.

His gambling had maxed out our credit cards, and the mortgage was unmanageable. We sold our lovely house, cleared the debts, and downsized to a much smaller house. I should have ended it then, but financial constraints held me back. One night, after a scathing bout of verbal abuse toward my son and me, words a child should never hear, I reached my limit. They were the most degrading I had ever heard him speak, I demanded he leave.

His response was violent, at first. He hid my purse and keys, preventing my escape from the house. In a frenzy, he pushed me around, threw objects, and banged my head repeatedly against the tiled bathroom wall. I stopped resisting, and he finally let go. I stayed in the bathroom, sobbing, while he went to bed.

The next morning, I confronted him when he was sober, he pushed me into walls again before packing and leaving. I documented the injuries with my doctor but didn't report him, fearing the repercussions on his job as a prison officer, we still had a mortgage to pay. Instead, I patched up the damage to our home and put it on the market.

The house sold, and my son and I moved into a unit, close to school and transport. After a few months, despite everything, I let my husband back into our lives once again, feeling sorry for him. It was a mistake. The cycle of drinking and gambling resumed. I finally said no more. That night was the worst. He chased me through the unit, smashing doors to reach me. In the garage, he strangled me until my son intervened. Once again, I told him I wanted him gone.

The next day, oblivious to his actions, he asked why I wanted him gone - WTF - he didn't remember what he had done . I lost my shit and just screamed at him to leave. Thankfully, It was school holidays and I had booked a unit for the week down the coast at Coollangatta. My son and I left, giving him a week to move out. He found a place, and we helped him settle in. We got along better apart, but the peace was short-lived. The abuse returned, and I was done. More threat of suicide, more promises but I was not being sucked back into his lies.

In October 2013, twenty years after our wedding, we divorced. There was nothing left to divide; he'd squandered it all. I took nothing from him, I wanted no more to do with him. My son and I lived in a rented house, trying to break free from his influence. Yet, he continued to make life difficult, refusing to let go. It was time for a new escape plan, a fresh start away from Brisbane.

CHAPTER FOUR

Escape from the Ex – How I Ended up in my First Rehab

The railway company I worked for had offices across Australia, and over the past six years, I'd been honing my skills in the supply chain profession while steadily climbing the corporate ladder. In September 2012, my manager offered me the opportunity to transfer to Rockhampton, in Central Queensland. It felt like perfect timing. Most of the projects I was involved with at the time were based between Rockhampton and Mackay, so relocating would simplify things for everyone. After talking it over with my son, we both agreed, it was exactly what we needed. He already had friends in the area, and the move promised a fresh start for both of us.

By December 2013, we were packing our lives into boxes and heading north. We found a rental in Yeppoon, a laid-back beachside town about fifty kilometers from Rockhampton. The house sat on ten acres of bushland, just five kilometers from the ocean. It was a sanctuary, four bedrooms, two bathrooms, two generous living areas, a chef's kitchen that seemed made for me and my love of cooking, a four-bay shed for the cars and, It also came with a beautiful resident peacock named Steve! Surrounded by nature and so close to the sea, I felt I was inching closer to my dream: living absolute beachfront.

The ocean had always been my refuge. It calmed me in ways nothing else could. Wandering the shoreline, barefoot and unhurried, collecting shells - that was my therapy. Out there, with the salt air in my lungs and the waves crashing against the sand, I felt completely at ease.

Moving day arrived at last. My son took the wheel of his own car, his best friend in the back, me in the front, him diligently clocking hours toward his driver's license, while my trusty Toyota Hilux 4WD was transported separately. It was an eight-hour drive, long and filled with his very loud music, but I loved every minute of it. The open road, the anticipation of change, it all felt like the beginning of something good.

We arrived on a Wednesday night, though we couldn't pick up the keys to our new place until Friday, the same day our furniture was scheduled to arrive. My son stayed with friends, and I checked into a motel on the outskirts of Rockhampton.

Since I was on holiday leave and it was close to Christmas, I accepted an invitation to a Christmas party hosted by one of my heavy machinery contractors. A lovely woman from their team picked me up from the motel around midday on Thursday, and we headed off to the celebration.

The party was held at a local golf course, a beautiful spread of festive food laid out buffet-style. The wine was flowing freely, and the atmosphere buzzed with laughter and holiday cheer. I started out drinking in moderation, knowing I had a big day ahead the next day, but as the afternoon wore on, I switched to vodka and Coke, trying to pace myself, though perhaps not wisely.

Later, the group moved to the local football club to keep the party going. It was conveniently close to my motel, so I tagged along. That's when I made a *very* poor decision: I switched back to wine. From that point on, things got blurry. I remember falling and skinning my knee on the carpet at the club, and then, nothing. The rest of the night vanished into a haze, a complete blackout.

The next morning, my alarm dragged me out of sleep in the motel room. I could barely move. My right knee had ballooned to twice its size, stiff and throbbing, while my left leg tingled uncomfortably. My eyeglasses were bent and scratched, and I had no memory of how I'd made it back to the room. I would have crossed a major highway in that state, how I wasn't hit by a car or truck is beyond me. It still gives me chills to think about it.

I called the lady who'd picked me up for the party, hoping she could shed some light on how I got home. She told me she'd left before I did and that I'd been very drunk when she last saw me. I was too embarrassed to confess the injuries I had from the night before. I just thanked her and left it at that.

Somehow, I pulled myself together. I got dressed, checked out of the motel, and drove the winding road through the bush to Yeppoon to wait for the removalists. My son and his friends met me there. They immediately noticed my limp and the angry swelling in my knee. I brushed it off, insisting I was fine. I wasn't. But I got through the day, moving boxes, directing furniture, pretending nothing hurt. That's what you do when you're trying to make a new start, you keep going, even if you're bruised, inside and out. My knee improved, but the nerve damage to my left leg lingered. Even now, eleven years later, I still have trouble sitting in some positions.

Ten days after the move, my son, his friend, and I made a quick trip back to Brisbane for Christmas. We planned to surprise a few friends. I stayed with my Mum, while my son stayed with his girlfriend's family. It was during that visit that they hatched a plan, he would move back to Brisbane and live with them.

The news quietly broke my heart. I wasn't ready to let him go, especially so soon after we'd started fresh in Yeppoon. But deep down, I knew it was the right decision. At that point, I was still drinking too much, stumbling through my own struggles, and I wasn't being the role model he needed.

There were clear expectations for him if he was to move in with them: he'd be treated as part of the family, expected to join in on outings, contribute around the house, and carry his own weight. He'd need to find a job, pay rent, and take care of his personal expenses. To me, it sounded like a dream come true. He'd be part of a stable, loving household, getting to see how a healthy family actually worked, something I'd always wanted for him, even if I couldn't give it myself at the time.

He flourished in that environment, they welcomed him with open arms, treating him like one of their own. Within two weeks of moving in, he'd landed a job, and today, he's their son-in-law and they absolutely adore him.

After my son moved back to Brisbane, the house I'd rented for us suddenly felt cavernous, too much space, too many echoes. It wasn't meant for just one person. I broke the lease and found a cozy little two-bedroom apartment, tucked much closer to the beach. It was part of a three unit complex with decor dating back to the 1960's, very quirky especially the orange and brown carpet. I made it homely, even adopting a cat for company! It didn't have ocean views, but the sand was only 100 metres away, just beyond a narrow path that led straight to the water. Another small step toward my dream of living right on the beachfront.

Still, the silence hit hard, I drank more, alcohol was controlling my life now. Loneliness crept in during the quiet evenings, and I was still finding my footing in this new town. But my job kept me grounded. I had a solid team, and my work took me on the road every week, between Rockhampton, Mackay, and the outback to the west. That rhythm gave me something to hold on to.

Every afternoon, after work, I'd head down to the beach, the sea became my sanctuary. On weekends, I'd take my 4WD and drive the long coastal stretch of Farnborough beach, wind in my hair, music up loud as I could, salt spray on the windshield. This became my favourite beach, and stretched for ten kilometres only ending where the dense bushland swallowed the sand. I'd park the car at the end and walk for hours, collecting shells like treasure. Those days were magic.

In February, my son and his girlfriend came up to visit for my birthday. I took them exploring, down four-wheel drive tracks in Byfield National Park and along the quieter beaches north of Yeppoon. Both of them were sixteen and on their learner's permits, so I let them take the wheel and drive along the sand. Watching them laugh, seeing my son so full of life, was a gift. He was thriving in Brisbane. Letting him go had been the right choice, I could see that now with complete clarity.

By April 2014, six months after my divorce, my ex-husband and I were still orbiting each other. We spoke now and then, never quite letting go. We danced around the idea of reconciliation, circling hope and memory. Alcohol convinced me it could work. That I could have it all, that he'd be waiting when I was ready, and somehow, everything would fall back into place.

I was delusional. But at the time, I couldn't see it.

I knew no one else in a new relationship would tolerate my behavior, even though returning to him meant a life of misery.

It still felt like the only solution, familiar pain, after all, was less frightening than the unknown.

He came to visit me in Yeppoon, considering a job at a correctional facility just outside Rockhampton. We spent the weekend together, and for a moment, things felt steady, maybe even hopeful. But the illusion shattered the moment he returned to Brisbane. He sent a text: he was seeing someone else. And it was serious.

That was when my world truly fell apart. I had clung to the belief, deep down, maybe foolishly, that we'd end up back together someday, even if it took twenty years. That hope evaporated with a single message. I was devastated; the pain in my heart felt like it was being ripped from my chest.

I grabbed a beer from the fridge (he had left some in there) and fled to the dunes by the beach. The sky was heavy with stars, the air thick with salt and grief. I sat in the sand, staring out at the water as tears poured down my face. The waves kept rolling, indifferent to my pain. I stayed there for over an hour, numb and broken, before I finally wandered back to my apartment. The silence was suffocating.

I was consumed by dark thoughts: *What am I going to do now? No one will ever want me, I drink too much, I'm overweight, unattractive, useless.* I spiraled fast, sinking into a despair so deep I didn't see a way out. I didn't want to live anymore.

The next morning, I went to the beach, hoping the water might soothe the ache, or swallow it. I waded out, deeper and deeper, I wanted to let go, to slip beneath the surface and disappear.

Then, clear as day, I heard a scream in my head. One word. My son's name.

It jolted me. Like lightning through my bones.

The cold water was suddenly sobering. *What am I doing?* The thought came sharp and clear, cutting through the fog. *How could I do this to my son? How could I do this to him?* He didn't deserve that, not after everything we'd already been through. I hadn't always been the best mother, but even thinking about abandoning him to ease my own suffering? That wasn't me. *No way, Jane*, I told myself. *Not like this.*

I turned and swam back toward shore. The waves pushed against me as if testing my will, but I kept going. When my feet finally hit the sand, I knew one thing with absolute certainty: *I needed help.*

But where was I supposed to start? I couldn't bring myself to tell anyone how bad things had gotten. I was too embarrassed. I couldn't confide in my family or friends.

The next morning, I went to work like everything was normal, even though nothing was. I knew what I had to do. My workplace offered an employee assistance program, something I'd used once during my divorce.

Hands shaking, I made the call. As soon as someone answered, the dam broke. "I need help," I blurted, and then the tears came hard and fast. I barely managed to get the words out: that I was scared, that I was drinking too much, that the thoughts I'd been having were darker than I'd ever imagined.

I was lucky. The woman who took my call had a background in alcohol and drug counseling, she knew exactly how to talk me down. Her voice was calm, steady, like a hand reaching through the phone. She told me gently but firmly: I needed to get into rehab. *ASAP*. There was no tiptoeing around it. This was serious.

The next step was terrifying. I had to tell my manager what was going on, that I needed immediate time off to go to a rehab and that no one could know where I was going. My heart pounded as I made the call, ashamed and vulnerable, but he was incredibly understanding. No judgment. Just support. He helped me arrange leave and even assisted in finding a suitable rehab facility.

We landed on an addiction treatment program at Brisbane Private Hospital. It was structured, reputable, and covered by my health insurance, so long as I had a referral from my GP. That small detail felt like a miracle.

Within days, I had a booking and a plane ticket. Just like that, I was flying back to Brisbane, this time not to visit family or celebrate anything, but to enter rehab.

It was something I never imagined I'd have to do. As the plane lifted off the runway, I stared out the window, stunned. I was devastated. But somewhere, buried beneath the fear and shame, was the smallest flicker of hope.

This was my rock bottom. **This is where you met me.**

CHAPTER FIVE

Life After the First Rehab – Sobriety Take One

Returning home from rehab, I find myself grappling with the loss of two major things: not drinking and letting go of my past with my ex. It's a double-edged sword. The intensity of these emotions is overwhelming; they are so foreign to me. I used to drink them away or try to fix things, but this time, I'm on my own.

With my doctor's help, I arrange coverage through medicare to see a therapist. I find a warm, soft-spoken woman who practices out of her home. Her office, nestled within her seaside cottage, is decorated in hues of ocean blue and sandy beige, with shells and driftwood arranged along the windowsill like offerings from the tide. The moment I step inside, I feel myself exhale, I'm immediately at ease.

I tell her everything, what has been happening in my life and what I am struggling to understand. Speaking the words aloud lifts a weight off my shoulders. Her response was gentle but firm: what I am experiencing was normal. With time and care, she assured me, things will get better.

We speak about cognitive behavioral therapy and mindfulness. She encourages me to explore my past, even the painful pieces I had sealed away, especially my former relationship, marked by domestic violence.

I resist, not wanting to return to that darkness, but she explains why it matters. Healing, she said, often begins where we'd rather not look.

She introduces the concept of Stockholm syndrome, and the comparison strikes a deep chord. It explains so much, why I had stayed, and even why I still felt drawn to him. Understanding that helps untangle my guilt from my grief. It also helps me to see why I drank during my marriage: it had been my only way to numb the confusion and pain. This insight became a turning point in my recovery. I feel a sense of release, as if the cords tying me to that version of myself had finally come undone. I don't need to drink anymore. I am free.

Embracing mindfulness, I take a chance on adult colouring books, something I'd once dismissed as silly. To my surprise, they were the best coping tool I've ever found. There is something soothing about selecting just the right shades, guiding the pencil carefully within the lines. Each stroke gives me a sense of control and calm, a small ritual that makes my days feel more manageable, even enjoyable.

During this time, I cry. A lot. Sometimes I sob like it is the end of the world. But these tears, heavy and hot, did more than sting, they cleanse. Once the hurt, the anger, and the sadness has poured out, I feel strangely whole. For the first time in ages, I feel like a normal person.

But as the fog begins to lift, the cravings creep back in, slow, sly, and familiar. I haven't yet tried Alcoholics Anonymous (AA). After rehab, I'd been prescribed Campral to curb cravings, but it didn't agree with my antidepressants making my mind so foggy and tired, so I stopped taking it. Left with nothing but willpower and worry, I turn to Google to find the local AA meetings.

I find the schedule and there are meetings held every Sunday morning in Yeppoon, so I decide to go to the next available one. The meeting is tucked away in a small room at the back of a hall, the kind of place you wouldn't notice unless you were looking for it. Walking in, I feel exposed and ashamed. To me, showing up to AA meant I'd failed. I

am terrified to be here alone, afraid of being judged and, if I'm honest, already judging everyone in the room. I'm imagining something bleak.

The room is set up in a circle, plastic chairs facing inward, people settled quietly, listening to someone speak. I slip in late, thanks to a time mix-up on the website. They are halfway through the meeting before I even sit down. I am unsure of what's happening or what I'm supposed to do. I just listen, but nothing really lands. It's like walking into the middle of a conversation in a language I don't understand.

After it ends, I hover awkwardly, unsure whether to bolt or linger. That's when a woman approaches me. She smiles, introduces herself, and hands me her number without hesitation. I'm floored by her warmth. That someone would notice me, a stranger, and reach out so quickly? It humbles me. I admit I feel completely out of my depth. She nods, like she's heard it a hundred times before, and says, "Call me anytime, just to talk."

That moment sinks into me. I don't remember her name, but I'll never forget what she did. It gave me something I hadn't had in a while: hope. She tells me there's another meeting that night, something about a "Big Book." I have no idea what she means, but I nod and say I'll go.

That evening, I walk into the same hall, only this time I head upstairs. The room is different, smaller, more intimate. People are gathered around a table instead of sitting in a circle. They greet me kindly as I take a seat, and then they begin reading aloud from a book I now know is the Alcoholics Anonymous "Big Book." One by one, they take turns reading and sharing what the passage means to them.

I try to follow along, but mostly I hear stories of relapse. Again and again. It throws me. People talk about slipping, starting over, and somehow it being okay. It doesn't sit right with me. When my turn comes, someone points to a paragraph for me to read. I do, then share a bit about my recent struggles and my decision to quit drinking. I speak honestly, but I'm still confused, lost, even.

Walking out of that meeting, I shake my head. No way. This is not for me. I don't want to hear about people failing and calling it progress. I've given up drinking for good, and I don't want that kind of negativity near me. So I won't go back.

I'm tackling this alone. One thing from rehab sticks with me: **ROUTINE**. It becomes my anchor, the backbone of my recovery. Training my brain to move through the day differently is essential, my survival depends on it.

So I create structure. Every morning, I wake up, get dressed, and head to work. My problem with alcohol was never during the day. It always started when I got home, when the silence crept in and the loneliness got loud. That's where I focus: the after-work hours.

I build a new ritual. As soon as I get home, I throw on my walking clothes and head to the beach. For an hour, I walk along the sand, blasting music through my headphones as loud as they could go. The heavier the better, Foo Fighters, Greenday and MCR, screaming guitars and chaotic drums help me let it out. I let the music drown out the noise in my head. I collect shells as I go, my little treasures, they ground me in the moment.

After the beach, it's time for a hot shower. Then dinner. Then dessert, always dessert. I plan it ahead of time, savoring the anticipation. It becomes my substitute for that glass (or bottles) of wine. My favourite? Tiramisu, heaped in a bowl and topped with whipped cream straight from the can. Pure joy. So good.

Then I unwind in front of the TV, letting my body relax. To ease into sleep, I use natural sleep aids, Rescue Remedy drops or tea with valerian, passionflower, and lavender. By 8:30 p.m., I'm in bed, soft music playing, book in hand, letting the words lull me to sleep.

If you think about it, drinking had a routine too. I had one. Every weekday at 4:30 p.m, right when The Bold and the Beautiful came on, I'd crack open that first bottle of wine. It'd be gone within the hour. Then I'd open the second and sip more slowly, as if that made it better. So really, this isn't so different. It's just a new kind of routine, one that doesn't destroy me.

Sure, life gets in the way sometimes, but the trick is always coming back to it. Don't let one disruption throw you off for good.

An amazing opportunity knocks, louder than I expect. One of my work contacts casually mentions a unit they have for rent, and it's totally beachfront! What?! My heart skips. This is the dream, the goal I've been quietly chasing.

"It's big," he says. "Two story, three bedrooms, two bathrooms, lounge, kitchen, and a balcony upstairs. Family room, another bathroom, laundry downstairs. Lock-up garage. And an inground pool. Thirty meters from the beach."

I don't even hesitate. My current lease is nearly up, and yes, it's going to cost me more, but I know I can make it work. I tell him I'd love to see it, and that very afternoon, I do. The moment I walk through the door, I take it. No second-guessing. It's perfect for me and Miss, my newly adopted cat.

The place is built of besser brick, rendered smooth and painted a rich, coastal blue. The master bedroom has its own private balcony that looks out over a soft green lawn, sloping gently toward the sea. The living room is wrapped in windows, offering a sweeping 180-degree view of the coastline, waves curling in both directions like an embrace, the smell of the salty ocean is sharp and invigorating, a briny tang that clings to the air and fills your lungs with each breath.

Downstairs, the living space opens onto a small courtyard with a gate that leads straight onto the beach path. Just to the right, the pool sparkles in the sun. Every corner of the place whispers peace and tranquility.

I've found it—my beachfront heaven.

CHAPTER SIX

The Romance Scam

Now that I've got a rhythm, I start thinking about what it means to have a "normal" life again. The truth? I don't like myself much at this point. I feel unlovable, unattractive, and convinced no one would want to know me, not really. But I push through that voice and give online dating a try.

It's...interesting.

I meet a few people, and as soon as I mention I don't drink, I never hear from them again. Still, I don't give up.

Then one day, boom! A message pings on the dating app from a very attractive younger man (fifteen years younger), and I mean *HOT attractive*. Right away, alarm bells start clanging in my head. Why would someone like *him* be interested in someone like *me*? But curiosity wins out. I reply, half-suspicious, half-flattered, and ask the obvious: "Why an older woman?"

He answers confidently, saying he's always been drawn to older women. He likes their maturity, their depth. He's not shy about it, either. It feels flattering, too flattering. Too good to be true. And, of course, it is...

Each time we arrange to meet, he comes up with an excuse and reschedules. Then he tells me he has to go overseas for work, to South

Africa, of all places. He says he runs a construction company and they've secured a contract in Johannesburg.

Another red flag.

And I ignore it.

He promises we'll talk every day while he's away. I agree.

The first time we speak on the phone, I'm horrified. No way is this the Caucasian man from the photos. I've heard this accent before, it sounds West African, maybe Nigerian or Caribbean. I'm thrown. I don't know what to say. So, stupid Jane just goes along with it. I don't question it.

He tells me he will be away for three months and asks me to take a chance on him, on us, I take the bait. I agree to wait for him to return to Australia so we can be together. I'm feeling vulnerable, insecure, and desperately in need of something warm, something real.

I fall into an online relationship with him, hook, line, and sinker.

Looking back, I see how I fell for every lie in the book. Love bombing. Sweet nothings. Promises of a future. He tells me everything I want to hear, and I soak it up like dry earth in a storm.

This goes on for months. And yes, you've guessed it, a scam. A long con, a romance scam, pure and simple.

When he finally asks for money, just a small amount, to buy medicine for his mother, I say no, he then accuses me of not caring, how could I not give him money to help his mother. Stupidly, I then say yes, not because I believe it entirely, but because I'm scared. Scared that if I don't, he'll disappear. That he'll decide I'm not worth his time.

I'm still tangled in the web from my past, still trained to please and not disappoint. The brainwashing from my marriage hasn't fully worn off.

One request becomes two. Then three. The amounts slowly increase, and each time he offers a reason just believable enough, usually something about his business or issues with equipment. He says he can't access his bank account, then gives me his online banking details and tells me to have a look. He insists he has the funds and promises to pay me back. I log in, and there it is: a balance of one million dollars. Oh my. Surely this can't be real.

I look up the bank online. It's a reputable American institution. Everything appears legitimate. But I still don't understand, if I can access the account, why can't he? I ignore my gut and keep giving. I want so badly to feel loved that I silence every red flag waving in front of me.

To get the money to send him, I start taking cash advances on my credit card, then small personal loans from those fast-money lenders with slick ads and sky-high interest rates. By the end of it, I've given him $40,000. Maybe that's small change in the world of romance scams, but to me, it's everything. It's every spare cent I don't really have. And I'm already carrying other debts.

People around me warn me, kindly at first, then with increasing urgency. "You're being ripped off," they say. But I don't want to hear it. I won't. That's how desperate I am to feel loved again. To feel wanted.

And it gets worse.

Deep down, I know something's off. I feel it in my gut. In my journal, I write: *I think this is a scam. I'm probably going to end up bankrupt.* But I keep going. Because in some twisted way, I've convinced myself it's worth it. I'm paying someone to say they love me, and that momentary glow, that illusion of connection, feels better than the truth. A tiny sliver of hope keeps me going. Maybe, just maybe, it's real.

The moment it snaps into focus is bizarre and almost comical. I get an email from him saying he won't call tonight so I can "rest up, have some chicken soup, and get better."

What the fuck?

I'm not sick.

Something breaks inside me. I stare at the screen and realize: *He's sent this to the wrong woman.*

I email back, furious. I tell him he's messed up, wrong girl, wrong lie, and I know exactly what he is. A scammer. He scrambles, saying he was "practicing" in case I *do* get sick. I can't even wrap my head around the audacity.

I tell him I know it's a scam. I demand my money back. He swears he'll repay me, insists he's not scamming me, says he loves me. I don't believe a word. Not anymore.

I know my money is gone.

He keeps emailing and calling, more empty promises, more fake affection. But I'm done. I've seen through the mask. It's clear now: the person in the photos isn't the person I'm talking to. The Skype video calls, always with a conveniently broken microphone, are just another excuse to hide his real voice.

I finally report him to the Australian Federal Police. It's the only thing I can do. If I can't get my money back, maybe I can stop him from doing this to someone else.

My world shatters. I'm heartbroken, once again. But this time, it's worse. I'm not just emotionally wrecked; I'm broke, completely, devastatingly broke. There's no light at the end of this tunnel, just the looming weight of debt, tens of thousands of dollars gone, sent to a man who never even existed.

I remember standing in the supermarket with exactly $45 left until my next pay. How do I feed myself and my cat for the next seven days? I close my eyes, take a shaky breath, and make the choices. Cat food, baked beans, bread and eggs. That's it. I check out and head home, feeling small and hollow.

It's time. I finally admit to my family and friends what they've probably suspected all along: I've been scammed, and now I have nothing left. I confess the truth, and it's like peeling off my own skin.

My Mum, my rock, doesn't say, *I told you so*. She just listens. Then she quietly transfers enough money into my account so I can pay the next week's rent and buy groceries. Thank God for her, she doesn't shame me. She just shows up, like she always does.

Then I break. I cry——no, I howl. Animal sounds, raw and uncontrollable. I cry for a week straight, curled up in my bed and empty inside. When the tears finally dry up, I do what I always do: I start looking for a way forward.

I manage to find a financial assistance program willing to help consolidate my debts so I can survive. The price? A five-year binding contract. I'm now one step from bankruptcy. The government gets notified. I'm banned from applying for any credit, even if I pay off the contract early. No credit cards, no loans. Just restrictions and shame.

I have to pay back $40,000.

And the worst part? I never spent a cent of it on myself or my family. Not one dollar. It all went to a lie. It crushes my soul.

The weeks that follow are bleak. I don't cope. I slide into a deep, choking depression. I lose faith in people, I stop trusting everything. I decide love isn't worth the pain. I feel like a fool, used, stupid and unlovable. I hate myself. I hate my life. I hate *feeling* anything.

This man, this scam, has stolen more than money. He's taken my hope. My energy and my will. I don't want to breathe, I just want to sleep and never wake up.

I start writing some very dark things in my journal, things that scare me. I reread them and worry for myself.

If there were ever a moment I might drink again, this would be it. But I don't. I won't. I refuse to let this idiot drag me back into that hole. I've worked too damn hard.

On April 27, I write a plea for help in my journal. It pours out of me, raw and desperate. *I don't want to feel this way, a good day is one where I don't feel like ending all of this, I have no pride, self esteem, no faith in myself, I'm just so fucking sad.* **HELP ME.**

What happens next? It is like the universe has answered my call for help.

The company I work for announces they're relocating my position back to the Brisbane office. I'm told I'll need to reapply for my own job. Just like that, it looks like I'm moving back to Brisbane. I keep my head down, focus on work, and cling to my routine like it's a lifeline.

A few weeks later, I interview for my role, and a week after that, I get the call, I got it. Relief washes over me. It's time to pack up and go home. My heart feels lighter for the first time in months. My family's thrilled, I can hear the excitement in their voices when I tell them the news.

By the end of July 2015, I've said goodbye to the beach, the sand, the ocean, the salt, the sea air that healed me in ways nothing else could, and I'm back in Brisbane. I feel a pang of sadness as I leave that chapter behind, but being near my family and friends again feels like returning to solid ground.

I move into a charming apartment close to the city. Big windows. Morning light. A space that feels fresh, full of possibility. I dive back into work and slowly start rebuilding.

Then, because I'm apparently a glutton for punishment, I dip my toes back into online dating. Oh God, what am I doing? I chat with a few men, meet a couple for coffee, but it's mostly them wanting to jump into bed rather than a relationship.

Then, out of the blue, a young man messages me. Immediately, my guard slams up. *Oh no. Not again.*

We start talking. I give him the third degree, grilling him about everything, sniffing out any red flags. I'm not falling for another scam. No way. But he's patient. Genuine. Kind. Eventually, I agree to meet him for coffee.

And would you believe, it's not a scam. He's a lovely man, easy to talk to and thoughtful. We become instant friends.

And then, somehow, despite the odds and the age gap (he's 21 years younger), we start dating. He's warm, affectionate, and present. He makes me laugh again. Out of all of the men I have been chatting with, this one genuinely cares enough to ask about me, wants to get to know ME. My family meets him, and surprisingly, they like him too. One day turns into another, and after a few months, he moves in with me.

We're building a quiet, happy life together. And after everything I've been through, it feels nothing short of extraordinary. Another lovely surprise comes my way this year in September. I am going to be a grandmother WOW. This is amazing—-life is great.

Another year is done and February 2016 is approaching, a major event is coming up, I am turning fifty!!!

To celebrate, I book a ten-day cruise from San Francisco down the coast of Mexico. No parties, no fuss, no clinking glasses filled with temptation. I want something different. Something peaceful. My partner can't make the trip, so I invite my Mum to come along. She's thrilled, and honestly, I can't think of anyone better to share this milestone with.

We sail past sun-drenched coastlines and sip coffee on deck as the sea stretches endlessly around us. The air is warm, salted, and alive. I spend my spare money not on wine or cocktails, but on spa treatments, facials and massages, tiny luxuries I once denied myself. Celebrating my fiftieth birthday on the ocean, is the perfect place, my happy place, my soothing place. I buy little gifts for my family and treats for myself, because I'm worth it now. I don't even think about drinking. I feel calm. Present. Free.

After two weeks of bliss I am back to reality and my ex-husband invades my life once again. He wants to talk. Against my better judgment, I agree. He's still bitter, still being nasty, still holding on to the past like it owes him something. Meanwhile, I've moved on. I'm happy. He's had other relationships, but from what I've heard, nothing has changed. The way he treats women, it's the same old story. I ask him just to leave me be and sort his life out.

Then October comes.

I get the call.

At first, I don't believe it. I can't. My ex-husband has taken his own life. He's said he would do it before, countless times, during and after our marriage. But this time, it's real. It's confirmed. He's gone.

And the timing? It couldn't be worse. It's two weeks before our son's wedding.

The grief is sharp and disorienting, but what hits me harder is the anger. How dare he do this to our son? Right before the happiest day of his life? I can't make sense of it. I try, but the reasons slip through my fingers like sand.

All I can do now is show up. Be steady. Be present. I don't dwell, not publicly. Out of respect for those who are grieving for their loss. I carry my own feelings quietly.

And then, as if the universe hasn't tested me enough, a week after his death, my partner ends our relationship. He says it's so I can focus on supporting my son, my daughter-in-law, and my grandson. I am truly grateful for him, I need to be with my family now more than ever.

We pack up. I leave the apartment, and he moves on. I move in with Mum again while I piece myself back together.

Once again, I rebuild.

CHAPTER SEVEN

My First Relapse

It's 2017, and I'm still sober. I'm living at home and settling into a new transition role at work, one that's meant to lead to a management position. Life feels solid. Hopeful, even. I've booked another holiday with my trusty travel companion, Mum. We're setting off in May.

Then, out of nowhere, everything shifts. My step-uncle, fit, cheerful, in his early sixties, dies suddenly in his sleep. I've just turned fifty-one, and this unshakable thought settles into my chest: *What if I die without ever having another drink?* It's bizarre. I know it is. But that's where my mind goes.

When May arrives, so does the excitement. We're off on a three-week adventure: first stop, Vegas. Then we hit the open roads of the Wild West, climb through the Canadian Rockies, and end with a seven-day cruise through Alaska's icy majesty. It will be stunning. But that thought still hovers in the background like a shadow: *Surely I'm cured by now. Could I have a drink? Just one?*

Trouble finds me at the international airport, tucked among the glossy displays of duty-free. A shop assistant offers a sample of a new liqueur. It's just a tiny glass. I think, *Why not? One sip won't hurt.* I raise it to my lips, I take that sip. It's sweet, smooth, then I drink the rest.

Mum sees me and gasps. "Jane! What are you doing? You can't have that!"

I laugh it off. "I'm fine," I tell her, too breezy. And I feel fine. I'm not craving anything. It doesn't even register that I've already broken the one rule that matters most: *I can't have just one drink.*

We board the plane, and luck is on our side—we were successful in our bid to upgrade to premium economy for just a few hundred dollars. It feels like a treat, a reward. I settle into my spacious seat. A flight attendant offers a choice: wine, orange juice, or sparkling water. I go for the water, guilt still prickling from the airport. I tell myself that one slip doesn't mean anything. Not really.

The flight is smooth. Relaxed. There's space to stretch out, snacks to graze on, drinks within easy reach. I feel calm, almost proud that I've resisted the wine. We land in Los Angeles, then catch our connecting flight to Las Vegas. The adventure continues. But something has already begun to unravel.

After a short flight, we touch down in Las Vegas. What a place, loud, oversized, and blazing with light. Everything here glows and pulses, even in the middle of the day. Neon signs flicker like electric confetti. The buzz in the air feels like caffeine and chaos.

We're staying at the Luxor, the hotel shaped like a massive pyramid. I'm giddy. Ever since I was a kid, I've been obsessed with ancient Egypt. It's the only thing I ever got a ten out of ten for in school, an assignment in Geography about pharaohs and pyramids and the flooding of the Nile. Stepping into the Luxor feels like walking into that childhood dream: dark hallways lit with golden sconces, hieroglyphs carved into the walls, statues of Anubis standing sentinel. I'm in awe.

We have three days here before the next leg of the journey. I've planned something special for the first day, a sunset helicopter tour into the Grand Canyon, complete with a picnic. We lift off from a small airport, sweeping over the Hoover Dam, the desert unfolding beneath us in dusty golds and rust-reds. As we descend into the canyon, the rock walls blaze with colour, crimson, copper, ochre, the depth is inconceivable, It's breathtaking.

We land on a plateau, remote and silent, with a view that swallows the horizon. Our picnic basket waits. I've pre-ordered everything: a light meal, two small bottles of sparkling water, and two tiny bottles of champagne, just for Mum.

But when I open the basket, it hits me like a punch to the gut, no water. Just four miniature bottles of champagne, glinting in the sun like treasure.

My heart stutters. *Should I?*

The voice in my head starts whispering, smooth and familiar: *You need something to go with your food. You're celebrating. You've done so well. Just one. One proper drink. What's the harm?*

That seed I planted weeks ago, the one about not dying sober—has sprouted into something twisted and persistent. I hesitate for a breath, maybe two.

Then I hear myself think: *It's been three years. You've got this. You're stronger now.*

I twist the little plastic cork, the tiny *pop* almost lost in the wind. The bubbles fizz, I pour it into the plastic cup. I raise it to my lips and take a sip.

The taste is sharp, cool, golden. Oh, it tastes **amazing**.

The moment that champagne hits my taste buds, I nearly cry tears of joy, of longing, of something I don't want to name. I'd forgotten how much I missed that crisp, golden taste. Every sip floods me with warmth and ease. Bliss sweeps through me like a wave, and for a little while, everything feels perfect.

I keep it to myself. No one notices. As far as anyone knows, I'm sipping sparkling water. I feel a flicker of guilt, but I shove it aside. I want this moment. I've earned it, haven't I? Just this one little bottle. That's all. Nothing more.

But this is it. The beginning of my first relapse. What I'll later call my "Three-Year Bender."

We climb back into the helicopter, and as we rise from the canyon floor, the sun begins to dip behind the red cliffs, setting the sky ablaze in orange and violet streaks. The Colorado River snakes below us, catching the light like liquid fire. It's a breathtaking end to a complicated day. I'm full of joy, and also something else, guilt, weighing heavily on my heart .

We spend two more days exploring Vegas, I am loving this vibrant city.

From Vegas, we fly to Salt Lake City to join the next leg of our journey, a bus tour that will carry us through the Wild West and on into Canada. For the next two weeks, we wind through landscapes that look like postcards brought to life: Yellowstone National Park, where the ice begins to melt in glistening sheets beneath a spring sun; historic battle sites like Custer's Last Stand at Little Bighorn; places with names like "Smashed-In Buffalo Head Jump," raw and vivid with history; and the stern faces of Mount Rushmore, carved into the mountain like gods.

Crossing into Canada is easy. We stay on the bus while our guide takes our passports inside to be stamped. Soon we're on Canadian soil, rolling into Calgary, where we stop at the site of the Winter Olympics where we take photos with the famous Jamaican bob sled. It's all clean lines and open sky.

Our next destination is the Columbia Icefield. It's cold when we arrive, sky flawless and blue, the air crisp enough to sting. Our excursion today is to walk on the glacier and the only way to get there is by a specialized monster of a vehicle called the Ice Explorer. It lumbers up the ice like something out of a science fiction film.

Once everyone's safely on the glacier, the tour guide calls us together. He pulls out a bottle of whiskey, his "special stash," he says, he has saved it for the first group of the season, us. With ceremony, he pours each of us a small shot into a plastic cup. The air is sharp, the ice dazzling white beneath our feet, a perfect day.

I take my cup.

Mum looks at me with a look that cuts deeper than any harsh word could. Her eyes say everything: *Don't do it.*

But I do.

I lift the cup. I drink.

And with that second drink of this holiday, I slip a little further away from the version of myself I've fought so hard to become.

The whiskey is smooth, surprisingly warm and delicious. I don't even *like* whiskey, not really. But this one feels different, like it was made to seduce. I sip it slowly, letting it burn gently down my throat, and that familiar fuzz starts to creep in around the edges of everything. The cold air feels softer. My limbs are a little looser.

Mum and I pose for photos on the glacier, sitting on bright red deck chairs stark against the white ice, laughing, then pretending to stumble like drunks in the snow. It's all in good fun, at least on the surface. The group joins in, everyone chuckling, the wind whipping our scarves as we slip and slide, bundled up like snowmen.

The guide comes around again, bottle in hand, offering refills. And of course, I accept. Why wouldn't I? That voice inside me, so reasonable, so reassuring, says it's fine. I deserve to enjoy myself. I've got this under control. *Still just having fun.*

From there, the tour winds deeper through the breathtaking beauty of Canada. We pass through Banff, with its fairy-tale charm, then on to Lake Louise, where turquoise water mirrors snow-dusted peaks like a painting too perfect to be real. We climb over the Rocky Mountains, each bend in the road offering views more spectacular than the last.

One morning, we spot a mother grizzly with her cub padding along a trail just beside the highway. It feels like a gift, raw, wild, unforgettable.

Vancouver is our final stop on the bus tour, a city wrapped in sea and skyline. The next morning, we step aboard a massive cruise ship, ready to sail north through the Inside Passage. Seven days bound for Alaska, where icy cliffs meet open ocean and bald eagles circle overhead.

The cruise is unforgettable, for all the right and wrong reasons.

Our first stop is Ketchikan. I choose a boat excursion to go whale watching while Mum stays on board, she's already done it on a previous cruise here. It's incredible. We watch humpbacks bubble-net feeding, their massive bodies rising through rings of foam like sea monsters from a myth. They surge through the water with a grace that belies their size, mist spraying from their blowholes into the crisp Alaskan air. Later, we motor past scattered little islands, and to my astonishment, we spot a bear and her cub wandering the shoreline looking for their next meal.

Evenings on the ship are a novelty for us. The sun still hangs high in the sky at 10:00 p.m., a strange sensation for us Aussies. Each night we dine in the restaurant, and the food is nothing short of sensational. Mornings begin with breakfast in our cabin, gazing out over the icy ocean, scanning the horizon for any flicker of sea life. On sea days, we take lunch out on deck, soaking up the cool Alaskan sun. I indulge in the onboard spa: massages, facials, body scrubs, spoiling myself thoroughly and without apology.

Our second stop is Icy Strait Point. We spend the morning on a local bus tour of the town and browsing for trinkets to take home. We duck into a local pub for a hearty Alaskan lunch, comfort food with a wild edge, then I have signed up for yet another tour, and this one isn't for the faint-hearted. I ride the world's fastest zipline, adrenaline surging through me as I soar above the treetops, the wind roaring in my ears, the vast forest a blur beneath my feet. I land exhilarated and buzzing. We return to the ship to set sail for our final shore stop, Juneau.

This stop we embark on the best tour of the entire cruise. We make our way to the local airport, climb into a chopper with a handful of other passengers, and lift off. We're going husky sledding.

The helicopter slices through crisp Arctic air as we soar above snow-draped mountains. The landscape sprawled beneath us looks like it's been pulled straight from a nature documentary, frozen lakes so vividly blue they almost glow against the endless white. Jagged peaks rise and fall like the folds of a giant, frostbitten quilt. For twenty minutes, it's pure magic in motion.

We land at the husky camp, and the excitement hits all over again. The dogs are already harnessed to the sleds, tails wagging, paws dancing on the snow-packed ground. They're ready. So are we.

The guides give us a quick demo, shows us the ropes, and then we're off. Mum sits on the sled, wrapped in layers, while I stand at the back, gripping the frame like my life depends on it. The lead driver gives the signal, and the dogs surge forward. And wow, they are *fast*. Wind stings my face, the sled bumps along the icy track, and all I can hear is the rhythmic pounding of paws and the creak of runners on snow.

We loop through a dedicated course, the mountains looming around us like silent spectators. Between rides, we tour the camp, where the handlers live, where the dogs sleep. Everything is rugged and raw, and it looks *cold*. Brutally cold. But there's a strange beauty in it, too.

Once everyone's had their turn, we pile back into the chopper. The return flight is every bit as breathtaking as the first, the landscape glowing under the late Arctic sun. What an experience, absolutely unforgettable.

As a final treat on our return to Vancouver, we cruise around the mighty Hubbard Glacier. The ship opens its front deck so we can get as close as possible. It's freezing, but absolutely worth it. The wind bites at our cheeks, sharp and clean. The glacier groans in the distance, a deep, ancient sound, as if the earth itself is shifting. Massive blue shards crack and tumble into the sea with a thunderous roar. It's wild. Raw. Hypnotic.

To make the experience even more special, the bar staff come around with trays of hot chocolate, laced with Baileys Alcoholic Irish Cream, and served in these cute thermal mugs we get to keep as souvenirs. Of course, you guessed it: I buy one. And I drink it. Every sweet, creamy, comforting sip.

It's delicious. And yes, I feel that familiar spark of guilt, but I push it aside, like I've been doing. *Just a little Baileys,* I tell myself. *It's part of the experience. It's fine.*

I'm still living in the illusion that I've got this under control. That I can have these drinks and somehow everything will still be okay.

But something inside me knows… I'm slipping.

The final day of the cruise arrives. We disembark in Vancouver and spend the day exploring the stunning city, soaking in its beauty before catching a train out to the airport for our flight home. And score! We win another upgrade to premium economy for the flight to Brisbane. I behave myself, no alcoholic temptations this time. Our holiday of a lifetime is over, and as we board the plane, I'm left with a deep uncertainty about what comes next.

Back home in Australia, reality settles back in, but I'm restless. I decide to move closer to work, into the heart of the city. I find a lovely little apartment with views of the skyline and the story bridge, with just enough space to feel cozy but free. It feels like a fresh start. A new phase. And I'm on my own again.

That little voice starts whispering: *You can handle it now. Just like everyone else. One or two won't hurt.*

I listen.

I tell myself that avoiding wine is the trick, that wine was the problem, not me. So I buy a sweet liqueur, something gentle, something

I can sip slowly after work. Just a small glass to unwind. A reward at the end of the day.

Then, I allow myself a glass of red with dinner. *I don't even like red that much,* I reason. *That'll help me drink it slower.* I feel almost smug about it. I'm proud, in a deluded sort of way, convinced I'm keeping everything in check.

But the more I drink, the more I chase that fuzzy feeling, that warm, numb wash I've missed more than I care to admit.

One night, after a few glasses of red, I think, *Why not white?* I always preferred white, after all. *I can handle it.*

That's the moment the slow unravel begins.

Within six months of that first sip on holiday, I'm fully back in it. Not just the occasional glass, but drinking, properly drinking. Heavily, and still, I tell myself, *If it gets out of hand, I'll just stop. I've done it before. I know how.*

But when it *does* get out of hand, I can't stop.

Worse, I don't want to. Alcohol has control of my life once again.

CHAPTER EIGHT

My Three Year Bender

Now that I'm back to drinking every night, I don't want to be sitting at home alone with my wine. I want company. Movement. Distraction. A friend tells me about a Meetup group for singles, people like me who go out to clubs, have dinners, dance, and drink. I jump at it.

And I love it. Instantly.

Before heading out, I have a few wines at home, just enough to take the edge off, so I don't have to spend too much at the bar. That's the plan, anyway. The music, the lights, the energy, it's electric. I meet some lovely people, and one woman in particular becomes a fast friend. We start going to everything together, Friday night dinners, Saturday nightclubs, every weekend is a party. We're having a ball. I'm fifty two years old, behaving like I'm in my Twenties, and loving it.

I'm well and truly in it now, on my bender, no question. And by the time I start thinking *maybe I should slow down*, it's already too late. The grip is tight. The willpower? Gone. I shrug it off. *Well, this is my life now*, I tell myself. And I keep going.

But my behavior is spiraling. Nights out become messy. I start drinking to blackout. I meet people that I put my trust in who may have not deserved it. I'm lucky, truly lucky, that I come out of those nights unharmed.

Getting home in one piece becomes a challenge in itself. One night, getting off at my bus stop, I fall out of the bus and land hard on my arm, cutting it open badly. One other time, I trip into a gutter, scraping my hands and knees and bruising my thigh so badly it turns black. I feel embarrassed, but it doesn't last. By the next day, I've brushed it off. I stop caring.

Self-esteem? That is slipping fast.

Each morning after a night out, starts with the same ritual: I check my body for bruises, then check my phone for photos to see where I ended up the night before. Sometimes I laugh it off. Sometimes I stare at the screen, not recognizing the version of myself in the pictures.

It's concerning—*I* know it's concerning. But I keep putting it off. Keep telling myself I'll pull it together soon.

Just not today.

August 2018, and I'm made redundant from my long-term job of twelve years. I start the job hunt straight away and pick up a short contract role, just four weeks, wrapping up early September. Around the same time, my final bonus cheque arrives from my old employer. It's a generous sum, part of my performance bonus from the past year.

With a little unexpected freedom ahead of me, I decide to make the most of it. I book a trip to the UK to visit one of my cousins for three weeks (I have been wanting to go for years). And right after that, I'm off on a long-planned getaway to Thailand with my bestie, and four other fabulous ladies.

The first leg of my flight to the UK is unforgettable. A day prior, I receive an email from the airline offering an upgrade to Business Class from Brisbane to Dubai for an extra $1,000, and of course I email straight back saying yes. How could I not?

Arriving at the international terminal, I make a beeline for the "First and Business Class" check-in counter, where I'm swept through with priority treatment. The process is smooth, almost regal. I feel like a VIP, gliding past the crowds with a kind of quiet satisfaction.

Duty-free sparkles around me, too many shiny bottles winking at me, I skip the temptation for now. I'll browse later in Dubai. Instead, I settle into the departure hall, anticipation humming just under my skin.

Then, the call: "First and Business Class passengers, please proceed to the gate for boarding." Yes! That's my cue. I'm on my feet, first in line, passport in hand like a golden ticket.

And just like that, I float down the jet bridge and up to the top deck of the aircraft, the pointy end, as they say. It's a whole different world up here.

From the moment I step on board, I'm swept into a world of luxury. We depart Brisbane at 9.00 pm., and I'm greeted with a cocktail of my choice as I settle into my wide, plush seat. A flute of Moët and Chandon Champagne, my new favourite drink, for takeoff. Warm peanuts. Linen napkins. I'm in heaven.

The cabin lights dim to a soft gold glow as the dinner menu arrives. I choose my meal, paired with a glass of white wine, and sink into the experience. This isn't just a flight, it's a floating hotel.

I'm flying with Emirates, on the majestic A380 Airbus, and to my delight, it has an actual bar at the back of the Business Class cabin. After dinner, curiosity, and a healthy buzz, pulls me down the aisle. And there it is: a beautiful, semicircular bar gleaming under soft lighting, barstools arranged neatly, curved lounges wrapped around the fuselage. It feels more like a chic hotel lounge than an airplane.

There are bowls of snacks on the bar, nuts, chocolates, chips, and bottles of wine and champagne chilling in silver ice buckets. One of the flight attendants is behind the counter, ready to mix any drink you can dream up.

I strike up conversations quickly. Everyone's relaxed, cheerful, tipsy. I find my tribe for the evening, especially one woman who's just like me: laughing a little too loud, soaking up every luxurious second. We're sipping Moët like it's water. I lose track of how many bottles we work our way through before deciding to pace myself with a couple of vodka, lime, and sodas, my other old favourite. I believe the saying is, one drink in the air is equivalent to three on the ground…ooops.

Eventually, a flight attendant gently tells us to keep it down. Apparently, we're disturbing the peace. That's my cue. I know I've crossed the line, again. So I say my goodbyes, wobble slightly back to my seat, and collapse into the comfort of a flatbed cocoon, blissed out and buzzed.

Morning arrives with a soft nudge and the aroma of hot breakfast. I sit up to a tray of eggs, fresh fruit, warm pastries, and I am offered another glass of Moët. I actually manage to say no this time. We're soon to land in Dubai, and I want to be alert enough to soak it all in.

At the airport, I make a beeline for duty-free. I browse the shelves with a specific mission: to pick out something "special", a beautiful bottle of alcohol to bring as a gift for my cousin.

Because of course, what else would I bring?

The next leg of the journey is from Dubai to Manchester, a short seven hours compared to what I've just done. I'm back in economy for this flight, but I've treated myself to a seat with unlimited legroom, so it's actually not too bad. I stretch out, relax, and before long, I'm landing in the north of England, where cool air and gray skies greet me for my next adventure.

At arrivals, my cousin scoops me up in a flurry of hugs, and we chatter like teenagers the whole way back to her place. I'll be staying with her and her family on their dairy farm in Gomersal—a stunning stretch of property nestled in the Yorkshire countryside. It's 100 acres of rich, rolling green paddocks, dotted with one hundred dairy cows and ringed by stone fences and leafy trees. Photos don't do it justice, you have to stand there, breathe it in, feel the wind on your face to understand its beauty.

Their home is just as impressive. A classic farmhouse with all the modern luxuries: a glass conservatory that soaks up the morning light, a roaring open fireplace, a spacious, stylish kitchen. And the best part of the kitchen? A wine fridge, built right into the end of the bench. Naturally, I clock it immediately.

We drop off my luggage and head into the local village to grab some groceries, and, of course, wine. I'm delighted by how cheap the bottles are, until I do the math and remember the exchange rate. Still, cheap is cheap, and I'm not complaining.

I pick up a few bottles, telling myself I'll keep it moderate. Just a couple, enough to enjoy. We stroll around the quaint little town, cobblestone streets, flower boxes in the windows, the kind of place that looks like it belongs in a film.

Back at the farm, the kitchen fills with warmth and the smell of roast meat and herbs. My cousin is busy whipping up a hearty meal, while I plant myself next to the wine fridge and make sure our glasses stay full, well, mine anyway. She doesn't have the same issue with alcohol that I do, and I admire that. Envy it, even.

Her youngest son surprises me by making the best Yorkshire puddings I've ever tasted, and he's only nine! Light, fluffy, golden little clouds of perfection. We gather around their huge family table, the kind you can lean on with your elbows and talk for hours. It's a proper welcome feast.

Later, we settle into the lounge with nightcaps by the fire. The flames flicker, our cheeks pink from wine and warmth, and the coziness of it all wraps around me like a thick blanket.

I'm staying in the guest room at one end of the house, a private little nook with its own bathroom. They get a lot of visitors from Australia, so it's perfectly set up. Comfortable. Inviting. I unpack a few things and sink into the bed, feeling at home already.

We've got a packed couple of weeks ahead, sightseeing, farm life, catching up. I've also planned a solo trip down to London for a few days, just me and the city.

The weather is surprisingly kind, it's autumn in the UK, and the air is mild, which is a blessing because I *hate* the cold. While the kids are at school, my cousin and I make the most of our time together. We explore breathtaking old abbeys and castles that loom with history, wander through underground gem caves that shimmer with mystery, and stroll through a sculpture park where art seems to grow straight out of the earth.

Then it's time for my solo adventure, I head down to London on the fast train, gliding through the countryside until the city's skyline rises to meet me. I navigate the Tube like a pro, dragging my little suitcase through the winding tunnels until I reach Westminster, where I'm staying in a charming little bedsit.

It's a top-floor attic room, three flights up, and the last staircase is so steep it comes with a rope for a railing. *Right,* I tell myself, *better take it easy on the wine.* Hmmm, not likely.

I drop off my bags, freshen up, and head out for some sightseeing. The city buzzes with life, and I find myself in a cozy pub just in time for happy hour. I order a wine, flip through the menu for an early dinner, and soak in the London vibe. Before heading back, I stop at a corner shop to grab a couple of bottles of wine for the evening. I arrive home and head up the stairs, with a rope climb at the end to my little attic, I settle in front of the telly, glass in hand, legs up, completely content.

The next day, London delivers a surprise, blue skies and a heatwave. It's going to hit 27 degrees Celsius, and I'm thrilled. This is *my* kind of weather. I hop on one of those big red double-decker buses and ride it all around the city, hopping off at landmarks and soaking in the sunshine. I stop for a delicious lunch (and yes, a sneaky wine) at Jamie Oliver's restaurant, then wrap the day with another happy hour at my now-favourite pub. That night, it's me, the rope climb and the attic, a few more wines once I am up there, and a view of London rooftops from the tiny window.

On my final morning, I stroll through Kensington Park, the leaves golden and crisp underfoot, before making my way back to the station. The fast train whisks me back to Leeds, where my cousin is waiting, all smiles. We head straight back to the farm for the rest of my stay.

The next morning, I'm in for a country-style treat, helping to milk the cows. Dressed in sweats and gum boots, I follow my cousin down to the milking sheds. One hundred dairy cows stare back at me, each with its own personality, lined up like seasoned pros. My cousin shows me the routine, how they file in, how to attach the suction cups to the teats, and let the machine do the rest. Easy, right?

Not quite.

I step up, suction cups in hand, ready to give it a go, and BAM! One of the cows kicks up her back leg. I *just* dodge it in time, saving myself from a broken face. My cousin? She's *filming the whole thing* and absolutely wetting herself laughing. I'm glad to provide the entertainment. Eventually, I manage to get the cups on and watch the milk flow. It's fascinating, but let's just say it's not a career move I'm rushing into.

For the last two days of my trip, more visitors from Australia arrive, so I move out of the guest room and into one of the boys' rooms. It's fine, until the first night, after a few too many wines, when I get up to find the bathroom, in an unfamiliar part of the house, the pitch-dark hallway.

Crash!

I trip on the hall runner and fall flat on my face. Right outside my cousin's door. OH NO. She swings the door open, startled, and nearly trips over me. She helps me up, points me in the right direction, and off I wobble on my merry way.

Yeah… it's definitely time to go home. Well sort of!, I won't be home for long!

CHAPTER NINE

Cheeky Monkey

Two days after getting home, I'm off again, another adventure calling my name. Thailand, here I come! I'm flying in with five incredible ladies, all ready for sun, sand, and cocktails. We touch down in Koh Samui, the warm air hitting us like a welcome hug, and make our way to our home for the next seven days: the luxurious Belmond Napasi resort.

The place is absolutely stunning, tucked into the island's lush greenery, perched right by the sea. We're each shown to our enormous villas, two of us to a villa, and it's like stepping into a dream. The rooms are decked out in perfect island style: fresh exotic fruit in bowls, fragrant flowers scattered artfully, and towels folded into elephants or swans on our beds. Everything smells of lemongrass and ocean breeze.

We quickly unpack and throw on our resort wear before heading down to the pool. It's late afternoon, golden hour, and we're greeted with our complimentary cocktails. We lounge at the edge of the expansive pool, dipping our feet in, sipping something fruity and icy while the sky melts into shades of coral and pink.

Soon, we're led onto the beach, where our welcome dinner is set up right by the water. Lanterns sway gently in the breeze, tables are dressed in white linens, and the sound of waves becomes the soundtrack to our first island night. Dinner is relaxed and delicious, sparkling water, a shared bottle of wine, and plenty of laughter.

One thing becomes clear quickly: wine is a luxury here. It's all imported and *very* expensive, like, eye-wateringly expensive. But maybe that's not such a bad thing. In fact, it might be the perfect built-in incentive to *not* go overboard this time.

For once, the price tag might actually help me pace myself.

The next day, we venture out to explore the local area. Another lady and I stumble upon a traditional Thai massage spot just a short walk from the resort. It's unlike anything I've experienced before. They walk on your back—yes, *walk*—then methodically work their way through every inch of your body, kneading muscles I didn't even know I had and then—-they massage my entire chest area! Whoa, steady on there lady, it's a bit of a shock but, It's oddly invigorating and deeply relaxing all at once. That first massage quickly turns into a daily ritual.

Later, we all wander through the local markets, soaking up the colours, the scents of sizzling street food, the buzz of scooters weaving through the crowds. We browse through stalls of sarongs, spices, and trinkets before finding a quiet beach where we settle in with chilled drinks and a lazy lunch by the sea. Every afternoon back at the resort ends the same way: mandatory sunset cocktails by the pool, golden hour casting a warm glow over everything. Then it's either dinner at the resort or we head back into town to chase down more traditional Thai fare.

On our third day in Koh Samui, we set off to tour the island's temples. Golden Buddhas gleam under the sun, towering over manicured gardens and serene courtyards. At one stop, there's a chance to have a photo taken with a monkey perched on your shoulder, an opportunity a few of us can't resist. The instructions are oddly specific: don't look the monkey in the eye, don't make any sudden moves, and keep your arm as still as possible. The monkey, tethered by a chain around its neck, is placed gently on my forearm. It all seems safe enough.

Photo's taken, the moment passes quickly and feels harmless, at least, I think so. What I don't notice until a day later is a tiny puncture mark on my forearm, where the monkey's claw must have scratched my skin.

After a full day of temple-hopping and monkey encounters, we return to the resort just in time for our beloved cocktail hour. The pool glows as the sun dips behind the palm trees, and we toast to another unforgettable day in paradise. It's an early night for all of us, we've got a big adventure planned for the next day.

We wake to a perfect tropical morning. Sunlight streams through the curtains, and the air alive with birdsong and the rustle of palm fronds. After a leisurely buffet breakfast at the resort, fresh mango, flaky pastries, and strong coffee, we gather at reception where our ride awaits: a rugged, open-air Jeep with bench seats bolted into the back for all of us girls.

No seatbelts, just a few metal bars to cling to, exactly my kind of fun. The other ladies eye the setup warily, white-knuckling their bags, but I flash them a grin and promise, "It'll be fine. Trust me."

And off we go.

From the start, it's a wild ride. The road turns rough, rutted with potholes, and the Jeep bucks beneath us like a mechanical bull. We jostle and laugh, holding on for dear life as we head into the jungle-cloaked mountains of Koh Samui.

Then, as if on cue, the sky opens up.

Rain pours down in thick, heavy sheets, drenching the landscape and turning the road into a muddy slipstream. Thankfully, the tour company anticipated this, and ponchos were handed out before we left. We fumble to pull them on, the plastic flapping in the wind, but it doesn't matter. We're soaked within minutes, rain dripping from our hair and pooling in our shoes.

And still, we're laughing.

The Jeep slides and fishtails around sharp bends, tires kicking up mud, and I can't stop grinning. The others squeal and clutch the rails, but I'm in my element, soaked, windswept, and loving every chaotic second of it.

Not long into the journey, our driver pulls over at a lookout halfway up the mountain for a much-needed morning tea stop. We climb out of the Jeep, stiff-legged and a little bruised from the bouncing ride and are greeted with a table of sweet Thai treats, flaky pastries with coconut and mango, that fill the air with the warm scent of fresh baked bread and ripe fruit, as well as hot tea or coffee served in delicate ceramic cups adding a rich, aromatic steam. The view is breathtaking. The island stretches out below us, a patchwork of green jungle, golden beaches, and turquoise sea, framed by a sky that's just beginning to clear after the rain.

It's a short stop, just enough time to sip, snack, and snap a few photos. Then we're back in the Jeep, resuming our bone-jarring journey toward the summit. The higher we climb, the rougher the ride becomes. By the time we reach the top, every one of us is shifting uncomfortably, rubbing our sore backsides and exchanging groans and laughs in equal measure.

But then we see it, the view. It feels like we've landed on the roof of the world. The sky opens in all directions, and we're treated to a full panoramic sweep of Koh Samui. Mountains roll into valleys, beaches hug the coastline, and the ocean sparkles as far as the eye can see. To me this moment is worth every bruise I will have on my body from the ride up here, seeing that vast ocean before me calms me as nothing else in this world can, I breathe in and savour the moment..

We're led to a small, open-air pavilion where tables are set for lunch. A traditional Thai meal awaits, lovingly prepared by a local family whose warm smiles make us feel instantly at home. The air is rich with the sweet, savory aroma of my favourite red curry, its creamy coconut undertones curling through the steam like an embrace. To our surprise, there's even wine by the glass, an unexpected touch of luxury atop this remote jungle mountain. We settle in, hungry and grateful, as dish after dish appears: fragrant curries, crisp-tender stir-fried vegetables, fluffy jasmine rice, and fiery sauces that set our taste buds alight. Every bite is fresh, home-cooked, and infused with care, the best food I've tasted all trip.

With full bellies and wine-warmed spirits, we wander around the summit, taking in the endless view one last time before beginning the descent.

The ride down is just as wild, slick, muddy, and full of squeals and laughter. We're soaked again, but at this point, it doesn't matter. We've surrendered to the chaos of it all, and it's become part of the charm.

Our final stop is an elephant farm tucked into the lush valley below. As we step from the jeep, we're each handed a small bundle of bananas. The elephants, massive, ancient-looking, and achingly beautiful, stand behind sturdy fences, their trunks swaying with a quiet patience. We approach slowly, palms outstretched, and they accept the fruit with surprising gentleness, their warm, rough trunks brushing against our hands. The moment should have been pure magic, yet it's tinged with sadness. These gentle giants are here to give tourists rides around the park, we were not aware of this part of the tour.

We want no part in that. None of us do. When the operator urges us to take a ride, insisting it's already included in our entry fee, we refuse again, this time making it clear that we don't agree with such treatment. "Please, respect our decision", we say. Our words hang in the humid air for a beat before we turn away. Climbing back into the jeep, we watch the elephants grow smaller in the rearview mirror. The day's tour is over, but the image of them will stay with us far longer.

By the time we return to the resort, we're muddy, damp, and thoroughly exhausted. Hot showers are non-negotiable. I stand under the steaming water, letting it wash away the jungle grit and the ache in my bones. After freshening up, we gather once more for sunset cocktails by the pool, a comforting routine now, and keep dinner light. Laughter still lingers around the table, but the energy is mellow tonight. Our comfortable beds are calling, and none of us argue.

I wake to another postcard-perfect morning. Sunlight spills across the floor, and the air outside is warm and still. No tours today, and thank goodness, it's our well-earned rest day.

But something feels off.

As I sit up in bed, a sharp pain shoots through my chest. I try to take a deep breath and can't. It feels like someone's cinched a belt tight around my ribs. Each inhale is shallow, strained. I wince and chalk it up to the previous day's wild Jeep ride, bruised ribs, maybe. A deep-tissue Thai massage should work it out, I reason.

Nope.

Even after the massage, the pain remains. It deepens as the day goes on, radiating through my chest like a fire slowly catching. Still, I press on. We've got plans, a trip to another part of the island for shopping, dinner, and something my bestie has been looking forward to the entire trip: a Ladyboy show.

We pile into a ride-share van and head out. The afternoon is slow and easy. We wander through town, poking into little shops and bartering for souvenirs, silk scarves, carved wooden elephants, handmade jewelry. The air smells like incense and street food, and there's music drifting from open storefronts. But I'm struggling to enjoy any of it.

The pain in my chest is constant now, gnawing and sharp, and I'm burning up from the inside. Every step feels heavier than the last. By the time we find a beachfront bar for cocktails and dinner, I'm nearly doubled over. I can't take a full breath. I sip water and smile weakly, trying not to alarm anyone, but eventually I have to admit the truth.

"I can't do this," I whisper to the group. "Something's wrong. I need to go back."

One of the ladies, my massage buddy, takes one look at me and stands without hesitation. "I'm coming with you," she says, already calling for a taxi. It's no longer a question of bruises or muscle strain. Whatever this is, it's something far more serious.

Back at the resort, my massage buddy shifts into full nurse mode. The moment we step out of the taxi, she marches me to my villa and orders me to put on my swimmers.

"You're burning up," she says. "You need to get into the pool. Now."

I don't argue. I'm far too sick to protest. My limbs feel like lead, my head is spinning, and the heat radiating from my skin is unbearable. I slip into my swimsuit and she walks me to the pool, guiding me gently by the elbow like I'm fragile glass. The water is cool and calm, a shimmering oasis under the fading light. I ease in slowly, the chill biting at my fevered skin. It's a shock at first—but also a relief. Immediate, soothing, grounding.

"You stay in there for at least twenty minutes," she says, standing watch like a lifeguard on duty.

After five minutes, I try to protest. "I just want to go to bed."

"Nope," she says firmly, arms crossed. "Stay. Twenty minutes."

I don't have the strength to argue, so I lean against the pool wall, eyes half-closed, letting the cool water do its work. Slowly, the fire beneath my skin dims. My breathing becomes a fraction easier. I'm still aching, but less so. And I start to feel a little more human.

When the time is up, she helps me out of the pool and wraps me in a towel. Her arm slips around my shoulders as she walks me back to my villa, steadying me like I might collapse. I tell her I'll be fine now, that she doesn't need to stay.

But she doesn't budge.

She settles me into bed, fluffs my pillow, tucks the covers around me, then pulls up a chair and plops down beside me. "Just sleep," she says, brushing me off when I try to argue again. "I'm not going anywhere."

I secretly love her for this. Her quiet determination. Her care.

While I lie there trying to get comfortable, she casually calls the resort kitchen and orders room service for herself. "I'm not leaving you alone" she announces to me.

I manage a weak smile. And then, finally, I close my eyes and drift into a restless sleep, still aching, still burning, but comforted by the fact that someone's keeping watch.

CHAPTER TEN

Lets Get Dry

Morning arrives, and with it, a wave of relief. I feel... better. Not perfect, but the fever has broken, the chest pain has eased, and I can breathe without wincing. Still, my energy is nowhere near adventure-ready.

Today's plan is a big one: a boat trip to nearby islands and a kayaking tour through sea caves. It sounds incredible, but I know I can't push it. I tell the ladies to go make memories, and wave them off from the edge of the resort driveway, doing my best to look more energetic than I feel. "Don't worry about me," I say. "Just enjoy every second!"

With the resort quiet and the day stretching ahead, I take it slow. I nibble on a light breakfast, some fruit, toast, and coconut water, then gather the essentials: towel, book, water bottles, and sunglasses. I make my way to one of the shaded cabanas on the beach, where the sand is soft and warm beneath my feet and the ocean sparkles like cut glass.

I settle in, stretched out under the canvas canopy, the tropical sun filtering through the palms. The breeze is gentle, the kind that carries salt and sunscreen and the occasional waft of someone's fruity cocktail. I spend the day doing exactly what my body needs: nothing. I dip in and out of the ocean, cool and clear, then return to my cabana to read, hydrate, and let the sun work its healing magic.

By the time the girls return, glowing and excited, their stories tumble out in a whirlwind, limestone caves, sea turtles, a pod of dolphins trailing their boat. I don't feel left out, only grateful they had the full experience. And truthfully, I needed this day to rest. I'm finally starting to feel like myself again.

That evening, I join them for our beloved ritual: sunset cocktails and a beachside dinner. We toast to good health, adventure, and friendship, the kind that insists you stay in the pool when you'd rather crawl into bed.

After a deep, uninterrupted sleep, I wake the next morning feeling whole again. The mystery illness, whatever it was, seems to have passed. I chalk it up to a nasty 48-hour bug and decide not to give it any more of my attention, for now that is…

It's our last day on Koh Samui. Time to pack, say goodbye to this island paradise, and head to the airport. Next stop: Singapore, for three more days of exploration, culture, and whatever surprises travel has left in store.

While we wait for our flight at Koh Samui airport, I do what any seasoned traveler would do, I wander into the duty-free shop. Not that I *need* anything, of course. Just a casual browse.

But then, displayed neatly on a shelf, I spot them: one-litre bottles of white wine. And not at outrageous airport prices, either. I glance at the label, the price tag, then back at the bottle. A grin creeps onto my face. I scoop up two and carry them to the register like I've struck gold. Future me is going to thank present me, especially in a city as polished (and pricey) as Singapore.

The flight is short, smooth, and easy. We arrive in Singapore and step into a wall of warmth, clean, tropical heat, thick with humidity but not unpleasant. The city feels instantly different: modern, gleaming, efficient. Everything moves with purpose, but there's an underlying calm. The air smells like orchids and asphalt, and there's greenery everywhere, climbing walls and spilling from balconies.

We check into our next hotel, drop our bags, and, as is now tradition, make a beeline for the bar. It's late afternoon and the skyline is just beginning to glow. We order cocktails, slide into cool seats beneath ceiling fans, and pull out our phones to map out the next few days.

Top of the list: Marina Bay Sands. The iconic three-pillared structure with what looks like a spaceship perched on top. We've all seen it in pictures, but now we'll see it in person.

Next, the Gardens by the Bay, a glowing wonderland of towering supertrees, light shows, and dreamy walkways suspended through lush canopies.

And to make sure we soak in as much of the city as possible, we decide on a big bus tour. The kind where you hop on, hop off, and let the city unfold around you, temples, hawker centers, colonial buildings, ultra-modern towers. No stress, no planning, just let the rhythm of the city guide us.

Every item on the list, ticked off, experienced, lived. It's time to head back to Australia. I'm exhausted, but in the best way. The kind of tiredness that only comes from something truly worthwhile.

But not long after returning from my holidays, I begin to feel... off. My energy disappears. I'm lethargic, my lungs ache, my body protests in every joint. It's eerily familiar, like Thailand all over again. This can't be good.

I book in to see my doctor. During the consultation, I mention I've just returned from two overseas trips, the most recent being Thailand.

"Any contact with animals?" he asks.

"Well... yes. A monkey. It scratched me."

His face says it all. This is not good.

He has to report the incident to the health authorities. I'll need to be treated for rabies, immediately. He makes the call. Everything is documented, and the health department arranges a course of vaccinations to be sent to the clinic.

The doctor hands me a leaflet outlining the complications. My eyes lock onto one line: *Rabies is fatal.*

Then comes the paperwork, blood tests for every virus imaginable. They need to rule out rabies, but I'll have to undergo the treatment either way. I take the leaflet home, pour myself a drink (I'm faced with the possibility of dying, what else can I do?), and start reading.

The next few months are rough. I don't have rabies, thank God, but I do have a serious tropical disease, courtesy of that damn monkey scratch. It's the type of sickness I have never experienced before and I never want to again

Still, not everyone can show they've had rabies shots, it is now on my immunisation certificate.

In the meantime, I was back on the search for a new job. It takes a while, and I finally land a fantastic supply chain related role with a large mining company. I will start with them in January 2019.

Eventually, life settles back into a rhythm: work, drink, party, sleep, repeat. But the drinking, it's dragging me down. I stop going out because I can't trust myself anymore. I'm getting too drunk, too often, and the fear creeps in. What if I don't make it home one night?

The hangovers hit harder now, what once took hours to shake off drags into days. Age creeps into the equation, and my body keeps sounding the alarm, warning me in ways I can't keep ignoring.

So I stay in. I drink alone now, getting close to drinking two bottles a night, every night, seven days a week, fifty-two weeks a year. Again.

By mid-2019, something finally clicks. I know I need to get things under some kind of control. Help arrives in a form I don't expect: my ex-partner and I decide to share an apartment together again. We both need support, just in different ways, and he doesn't drink alcohol. It's a blessing, for both of us.

We find a beautiful place, perched on the border of Fortitude Valley and Newstead, overlooking the city skyline. Floor-to-ceiling windows, warm afternoon light, and the buzz of Brisbane below. It feels like a fresh start.

Now that I've got everything else sorted, it's time to get my drinking under control. Once again, I turn to the support of my employer's help lifeline, the Employee Assistance Program, and book an appointment with a therapist, this time with one goal in mind: rein in the booze.

I walk in ready to fix myself. I explain my history, my past struggles, and what I'm hoping to achieve. The therapist listens and offers strategies to help curb my current drinking. I leave the session feeling hopeful, motivated. It's time to make a change.

I start by cutting back, and even sign up for *Dry July* to raise money for cancer charities, which means no drinking alcohol for the month of July. I kick things off with the best intentions. I will not have a single drop all month. Easier said than done. Every corner of my world is a trigger. The liquor barn downstairs, the pub next to it and the live music venue across the road. It's relentless. Glasses clinking. Music thumping. It's like being on a diet while living inside a bakery.

But there's a get-out-of-jail-free card: as part of *Dry July*, there's an option to purchase a *Golden Ticket*, a pass that lets you drink for one night if you donate. I've got a night out planned with a close friend, so I buy the ticket and give myself permission to let loose.

By the end of July, I've raised $500 and I'm genuinely proud of it. Only one night of drinking. I'm feeling good. Accomplished. The plan now is to keep the momentum going and limit my drinking to weekends only. And it works, for a little while, anyway. A couple of months pass, and then the old patterns start sneaking back in. Slowly, quietly, but surely. And before I know it, I'm spiraling again, back to drinking at levels that scare me.

Then came an unwelcome surprise, my job was being outsourced to Malaysia. What did this mean? Another redundancy! As soon as I received the news, I jumped straight into job hunting and, true to form, landed on my feet again (I really do feel like a cat). This time, I secured a similar role with a fertiliser company and I start with them in October 2019.

It's 2020—the year the world goes completely pear-shaped. "Coronavirus," as it's first called, starts creeping into headlines. I remember saying to my daughter-in-law in early January, "This sounds like it might become a pandemic." I say it half-serious, half-dismissing the thought. No way could it really get that bad. Could it?

But as the weeks tick by, the news grows darker. This *is* a global pandemic. The numbers of people infected climb and deaths are being reported. The panic spreads. It's like watching a slow-moving tidal wave build on the horizon. I remember hearing about the Spanish Flu of 1917, eighty million dead. And now here we are, over a hundred years later, bracing for our own catastrophe. It's not long before the world slams on the brakes. *LOCKDOWN.*

Everything changes. Social distancing kicks in. Stores and venues limit how many people can enter. Signs go up. Tape marks the floors. The air feels different, thinner, like it's holding its breath. By mid-March, life as we know it comes to a grinding halt. Shops shutter. Pubs go dark. Clubs fall silent. It's not enough just to keep our distance, we have to disappear from public life altogether. Thank goodness for my flatmate, we will be here for each other, I would hate to be living alone now!!

I'll never forget the date: March 16. That's the day I'm told I'll be working from home indefinitely. *Wow.* It suddenly feels real. Heavy. Serious. I pack up my office, monitors, files, paperwork, and haul it all home, setting up shop in the office nook of our apartment.

Now I can drink as much as I want after work. No random drug and alcohol tests, no alarms, no driving to site, I give myself permission to let loose. After all, the world is ending, right? We're all going to die anyway.

That's what my alcoholic brain whispers to me, handing me a twisted permission slip in the middle of the apocalypse.

Thankfully, I've never been a day drinker. I can hold out until 4:30 p.m. on weekdays. *The Bold and the Beautiful* becomes my unofficial alarm clock, when that familiar theme music starts, it's magic time. Pop goes the cork, and the first bottle of champagne fizzes to life. Hooray! This little ritual carries on for months, and honestly, I'm having a ball.

By mid-July, restrictions ease, and we're allowed back to work full-time. Time to reign the drinking back in, I will have to drive to work in the mornings and the random drug and alcohol tests will resume again. I'm classed as an essential worker, and I've even got the official letter that lets me travel to the site, like some kind of VIP. Back to the office I go.

But weeks of isolation have taken a toll. Champagne, rich meals (now that I have all the time in the world to cook), and absolutely zero exercise have done their damage. The scales don't lie, my waistline has officially declared war. On the flip side, staying in has saved me a fortune. No dinners out. No pub tabs. No impulse shopping. So what do I decide? A genius idea, of course: liposuction. Stomach and flanks. Why not?

A few Google searches, a handful of phone calls, and a month later, I'm booked in. The procedure goes well, (I wouldn't recommend it for the faint hearted, not if you choose to stay alert for the procedure), I feel lighter, freer, even happy again. But then reality slaps me across the face. It hits me: I've just spent a small fortune sucking the fat out of my body... and I'm going to put it all back on if I don't stop drinking.

I NEED HELP!!! Looks like I'm off to rehab—*again*.

PART TWO

The Second Rehab

CHAPTER ELEVEN

Déjà vu

It's now October 2020, and I know—I *know*—I have to go back to rehab. It's the only way I can stop. I've tried doing it alone, and I just can't. Honestly, this feels like the easy way out, but I don't have the willpower to go cold turkey on my own. I ask my doctor for a referral to see the same doctor who still treats patients at the clinic.

I'm admitting myself to the same rehab facility I went to six and a half years ago. I'm going back because it worked last time. I felt strong, centered and I stayed sober for three years. But my alcoholic brain, always scheming, convinced me I could handle it again on my own, flushing that three years down the drain. *Just one drink, it said. You're in control, it said.* Lies.

With my referral in hand, I call the clinic and book in for the following week. I give my manager the news I have to go to rehab, he is so very supportive and we quietly arrange my time off. There's no judgment, just calm understanding and the space to do what I need to do.

On the day, my flatmate drives me to the hospital. We pull up in another red hatchback, this time, a Hyundai Getz. And just like that, I'm hit with a wave of déjà vu. Same situation, same hope, same fear.

We stop outside the building. It looks different now. A new wing stretches across what used to be the car park, modern, sleek, almost inviting. I silently hope the rehab unit is in that part, the shiny new section.

I step out of the car. He grabs my suitcase from the back and offers to walk me in. I shake my head and say, "No, it's okay. I've done this part before." We say our goodbyes, brief, but full of unspoken love and comfort. I know I'll see him again soon.

Inside, the admissions area is nearly empty. Signs direct me where to sit. I take a seat, keeping my distance. COVID protocols are still in full swing, quiet, orderly, sterile. When I'm called forward, I give the admissions officer my name and explain why I'm here. No one's clicking a pen this time, which is a mercy. I'm hungover from last night's final drinks, and every sound feels sharp, I sign the paperwork. The plastic ID band snaps onto my wrist, the ritual is familiar, heavy and necessary.

The admissions officer points me toward the same elevator I took six and a half years ago. I am full of dread, here I go again, what a fall from grace. I step inside, the sterile smell of disinfectant hits me, I ride up to the third floor, heart heavy, stomach tight. But this time, the sign directs me to the new wing of the hospital. The rehab ward has moved. A fresh start, at least in bricks and mortar.

I find the nurses' station and let them know I've arrived for treatment. A nurse retrieves my file and walks me straight to my room. It looks almost identical to the one I had before, sterile, simple, but everything is newer. The paint is fresh. The bed looks clean and surprisingly comfortable. There's a small set of drawers, a private bathroom, and this time, a view: the Roma Street Parklands, lush and green, unfolding outside my window like a slow, deep breath. Soothing, if I let it be.

The nurse returns with the observations (obs) trolley. She wraps the blood pressure cuff around my arm, the same way they did all those years ago. I'm not as nervous this time. I know the drill. But beneath the surface, a wave of self-loathing churns. I can't believe I'm back here. Six and a half years ago, I stood in this same place, full of resolve, telling myself I would *never* return. And yet, here I am, sitting on the edge of this bed while she clips the oxygen monitor to my finger.

She asks how I'm feeling.

"Not good," I say, holding back tears. "I've been here before."

She nods gently. "It's okay."

But it's *not* okay. Not to me. I'm furious with myself, and I deserve every bit of it.

She finishes taking my obs and takes my blood for the mandatory tests. I'm starting detox again. She hands me a little white plastic cup, inside, the two familiar small Diazepam pills 5mg (millagrams each, my companion again for the next three days. I swallow them with a sip of water. Within minutes, that familiar floating sensation washes over me, softening the edges of everything.

Okay, I think. *Here we go again.*

The nurse explains the updated procedures. The rehab unit has expanded, now spread across two floors. The dining room is on this level, but due to COVID restrictions, we're not allowed to gather. No shared meals. No common areas. Everything, breakfast, lunch, and dinner, will be delivered to our rooms. I order my meals each night, ticking boxes on a form like I'm choosing from a menu in some joyless hotel. This is going to be a lonely two weeks, no relief from the crazy state of the world outside these walls.

The weekend passes in a blur of detox, foggy brain, I can't think straight and am so tired from the relaxing effect of the Diazepam. I have my laptop this time, so I binge a few TV shows, to distract myself. There's a television room, but it's off-limits for now. Honestly, I don't mind. I'm content to stay curled up in my room, steeped in regret. The shame sits heavy on my chest. I'm so damn disappointed in myself.

I receive the schedule with the classes to attend. Again, because of the restrictions, I won't get to meet anyone until the classes start.

Monday arrives, and I attend the first class. The program is the same as it was my first time, and it's the same therapist who took the classes last time I was here. I am surprised she is still doing the same thing, but I guess it is an ongoing problem and she wants to help us. This makes me feel hopeful.

This is the first time I get to meet the other patients. We introduce ourselves around the classroom, first names only, of course. I humbly say, "I was here six and a half years ago, and now I'm back." As we go around the classroom, everyone's got the same story, saying, "I was here six months ago," another says, "I was only here three months ago." "I come in all the time," "I come in once a year," this is not what I need to hear, my head is spinning!

The therapist hands out some photocopies of the training manual for us to read along with and take notes. She explains they're waiting on more manuals to be printed. We start working, learning all about pathways and cognitive behavior therapy. All exactly the same literature as I had six and a half years ago. After the class, as we walk out, I say to the therapist, "When will my manual be available?" She replies, "I'm not sure, but you'll get one next time you come." This really blows my mind! It makes me feel like I'm wasting my time here if she believes I will be back again, her words take all of that hope away. I take myself back to my room and ponder this.

Okay, Jane, you're going to do this. Don't worry about what anyone else says. Buckle down, do your two weeks here, learn what you can or relearn what you can. You know all of this. Let's get through it.

That afternoon, the doctor comes to visit, the same doctor who saw me all those years ago. Of course, he remembers me. I fill him in on what happened, why I'm back here, and how I'm embarrassed and ashamed to be here again. He's good about it; he must see this a lot, obviously. With everyone else saying they come every few months, he talks me through it. He also has my blood results, and they are exactly the same as the last time, enlarged fatty liver but all else is good. Yes I am still drinking that wonderful water.

Just basically, he says what I've told myself: buckle down, learn from my mistakes, take in as much as I can, and be determined to get through this. I'm in a much better state of mind. The only person I've got to blame is myself for getting back into this situation where I thought I could handle it.

They have a few different activities this time. You can go to a singing class with a few people, social distancing, of course. Music is fantastic therapy, and even though I can't sing to save my life, I join in anyway.

Mum comes to visit on the first weekend I'm allowed to have visitors. We walk over to the Parklands, just as we did over six years ago. We indulge in a lovely lunch at the café. How would I get through this without her? She is one of my biggest supporters.

On Sunday, my son, my daughter-in-law, my grandson and my granddaughter visit me, bringing a picnic blanket and a basket full of nibbles. We go across the road to the parklands, spread the blanket on the grass and have a wonderful picnic. They're so supportive of me once again, it is really uplifting to know they are here for me, I have so much love for them and I know I have been a disappointment.

I complete the next week of lessons and therapy, but I feel it is just not as serious as it was the first time around. I'm just so disheartened about the way people were so blasé about being there. One of the therapists said there's a fellow who comes in two weeks prior to going on a cruise to give his liver a rest and to detox.

Fourteen days later again, I walk out of there with mixed feelings.

My beloved flatmate picks me up in his little red Getz and we head home. I am happy to be getting back to my own surroundings, my comfortable bed, cat and just relaxing. The problem is, I am confused. I don't know why, but I decided to go downstairs to the liquor barn, buy a bottle of my favourite bubbles, and drink it. I don't feel anything except guilt. Now I am ready to stop… or am I???

CHAPTER TWELVE

Life After the Second Rehab – Sobriety Take Two

November 2020 and I haven't had a drink since that one crazy night straight out of rehab. I'm back in the rhythm of sober life, settling into the routines that holds me together. But something feels different this time. I call it *recovery fatigue.*

Every afternoon, like clockwork, I hit a wall, hard. Around 1:00 p.m., my body turns to lead, my eyelids droop, and my head pulses with a dull, persistent ache. Just walking feels like dragging myself through wet sand. All I want is sleep. Deep, uninterrupted, coma-style sleep.

What is this? I collapse into bed the moment I get home, a power nap, I say to myself. I chalk it up to the lack of alcohol, no more evening sugar surge, no more dopamine spike to prop me up.

The next two months drift by in a blur of work, naps, and sugar fixes, my beloved sweet deserts I have been planning all day.

As 2020 draws to a close, the holiday I planned to visit my cousin again in the UK is no longer happening, and I've received a full refund. With travel off the table for the foreseeable future, I decide it is time for a new car. I am still driving my Hilux, but no longer living at the beach, so a four-wheel drive isn't necessary for city life.

I've always dreamed of owning a luxury car, specifically a BMW, and conveniently, there's a BMW dealership just three blocks from my unit. One Friday afternoon in early December, I wander over to check out the pre-loved section. I spot two cars that catch my interest and are within my budget: a black diesel hatchback and a white sports sedan. After looking inside both, I decide to take the sports sedan for a test drive. It drives beautifully, so smooth compared to the Hilux, and it's automatic, with a sports button for that extra speed boost!

I buy the car on the spot, arrange to trade in my Hilux, and apply for finance. Now that I have paid my debt off, my credit rating has been restored, I can finally get my dream car. Five days later, I pick up my new pre-loved car.

Turns out, the upside of sobriety is this: all the money I used to spend numbing myself now goes toward things that make me feel *alive*.

As 2021 arrives, I declare this will be my best year yet!...That is not to be.

Two major events unfold this year, one good, one bad. My Mum fulfills her dream of moving to Tasmania, and I, unfortunately, let another wrong man into my life. This mistake unravels all the progress I have made over the last seven years!!!!!

Let's start with the bad.

Where do I begin to tell the story of a man who shatters my self-esteem, my confidence, and my sobriety? Were there red flags? Absolutely.

He's someone I know. We went to the same schools growing up, moved in similar circles, but never really crossed paths properly. This year, we reconnect through Facebook. A few messages turn into long chats, and eventually, we decide to meet up.

When I see him in person, he's not how I remember. Older, yes, but there's something else. A hardness around the eyes maybe, or just the weight of time. Still, there's a spark, a connection, and maybe I'm craving that too much, because I lean into it. Probably too fast.

We go out a few times. I feel relaxed around him, oddly at ease. We click easily, good conversation, easy laughs, a rhythm that feels natural. I start to think, *Maybe this could actually go somewhere.*

And then it all goes downhill. Fast!

One night, we're texting when I tell him a bit about my flatmate. I say he's from the Middle East, and the conversation suddenly shifts.

He replies, *"We can't be friends. I don't like how they treat their women."*

My stomach drops. The blunt racism, the ignorance—it's like a slap. WTF?

I block him immediately. No explanation. No conversation. Just done.

But a few days later, one of his friends messages me. He wants to apologize and against my better judgment, I unblock him.

I listen. He sounds remorseful, embarrassed, even. And I do what I've done too many times before: I give him another chance.

Because I want to believe people can be better. Because I want to believe *he* can be better. Because I haven't yet learned how much that kind of hope can cost me.

One night, not long after leaving my place, I receive another disturbing message.

"This isn't going to work. You live too far away and go to bed too early."

Seriously? WTF?

I block him. Again.

But here's the thing no one tells you: blocking someone doesn't erase their presence. It just muffles the volume.

I still see the missed calls stacking up like silent red flags. He calls over and over for the next few days, and eventually, stupidly, I unblock him.

Another apology. Another second chance. He's full of them.

When we're together, he's charming, sweet, even. He makes me laugh. But the second he walks out the door, it flips. Nasty messages start pouring in, all venom and blame. It's like he's split in two, Dr. Jekyll in person, Mr. Hyde in my inbox.

There is something deeply wrong with him. But the empath in me, the part of me still healing, sees a wounded man. And wounded men feel familiar. I think maybe he just needs love, patience and understanding. Would I ever learn?

Apparently not.

We keep seeing each other, on and off, for two more months. My journal from that time is a mess of confusion and justification, but one entry hits me hard when I reread it:

Blocked him again today. That makes eleven times.

Eleven. That's not just a red flag—that's a crimson parade.

I'm unraveling.

His texts are getting worse. I go to see yet another therapist, clutching my phone like evidence in a courtroom. I read her the messages aloud, my voice shaking:

"You're a maggot."

*"You're a c*nt."**

"You're cheating on me with your boss. Why? Because I went out to dinner with my team from work.

I sit there, heart pounding, shame rising up my throat like bile. The therapist listens calmly and then asks the one question I often ask myself.

"Why do you like him?"

All I can say is, "There's a kind side to him. When we're together, it feels real. It's after he leaves that everything falls apart. He's a keyboard warrior online, but in person, he's someone else."

I know how it sounds. I *hear* it as I say it. I sound like someone trying to explain away abuse. And maybe I am.

But in the moment, I can't quite let go of the idea that I can fix it. Fix *him*. That if I just try hard enough, love deeply enough, I'll break through the armor and find the version of him that shows up when he's soft and smiling and holding my hand.

Instead, I find myself shrinking a little more each day.

Between the recovery fatigue and the slow, relentless drip of emotional abuse, I broke.

I drank.

At first, it was just to take the edge off, to quiet the noise in my head, to soften the sting of his words. But it didn't stop there. I started telling myself I could control it this time, that I wasn't like *before*. That this wasn't a relapse, it was *management*.

But the truth? I was spiraling. Again.

For the next two months, it's the same vicious loop: I block him, I unblock him, I promise myself I'm done, and then I'm back, answering his calls, swallowing his apologies like sugar-coated poison. I can't seem to give up on him. And the more I try to make it work, the more I drink. A little more each week. Until the wine becomes ritual, comfort, escape.

My family sees it. My friends see it. They're watching me disappear behind my own choices, and they're begging me to walk away. They tell me I deserve better. That he's toxic. That I'm not myself anymore.

But I don't listen. As usual.

I've convinced myself that if I just *hang in there*, things will get better. That he'll change. That love will win. I read back through my journal entries from that time, and it's like reading someone else's heartbreak. I write about how much his texts hurt. How broken I feel. I promise myself, right there, in ink, that I'll block him for good.

But I don't even listen to *me*.

That stubborn, misguided hope, the part of me that clings to the idea of fixing broken things, just won't let go. I don't want to give up. I *can't* give up. Not yet.

So we carry on. Three more months of chaos. More fights. More apologies. More wine. By the end of it, I'm a shell, anxious, exhausted, unraveling. I'm back to drinking two bottles of wine a night, just to fall asleep without crying.

I am, quite honestly, a basket case. And I know it.

Finally, in June, I listen to reason and call it quits for good.

No more texts. No more unblocking. No more bargaining with my own self-worth.

Not long after, I book a ticket to Tasmania.

CHAPTER THIRTEEN

Drink Like There is no Tomorrow

Two weeks before I'm due to fly, I have an appointment to get the so-called *Covid vaccine*. AstraZeneca, because I'm over fifty and that's the rule. I check in at my doctor's clinic in the city. He writes the prescription, and I head upstairs to the registered vaccination center.

The needle is quick, almost nothing, and I'm told to sit in the waiting area for thirty minutes, in case my body decides to put on a show. The fluorescent lights bright overhead; the plastic chairs are cold against my skin.

After only a few minutes, a wave of dizziness sweeps through me, thick and disorienting. My stomach tilts. Is this a side effect, or am I just being nervous, or paranoid? I breathe through it, and it fades. Thirty minutes are up, I feel ok so I decide to head home and get ready for work.

But the moment I'm back at my apartment, the dizziness returns, heavier, almost tilting the room. My heart pounds like a bass drum in my chest. This is not normal. I call the clinic, my voice sharp, and they tell me to dial an ambulance immediately. My flatmate does it for me. Of course, if something can go wrong, it will. I'm Jane.

The paramedics arrive in a blur of teal uniforms and clipped efficiency. I tell them what's happening inside my body while they strap cold leads to my chest, check my blood pressure, and frown. Something's off. They treat me as if I'm having a heart attack. WTF has this vaccine done to me? I'm loaded into the ambulance, dread curling in my gut. Is this it? Am I going to die because the government says I need a green tick to enter a café? I always thought I'd go from alcohol, not an early grave courtesy of a preventative.

At the hospital, they wheel me into triage, take my details, then park me in a hallway queue behind a dozen others. I ask a nurse if something serious is happening. She glances at me and says, "Yes, all these people are having reactions to the Covid vaccine." Holy shit. That's not exactly on the evening news.

Hours later, I'm moved to a ward. My vitals are still high; my heart still thunders. Bloodwork comes back normal, but they say I need a heart stress test before I can leave. The person who runs it has already gone home for the day. Great. I'm staying overnight.

Around me, patients compare notes. A few have symptoms like mine, racing heart, dizziness, while others sport swollen limbs, ballooned arms, thick legs. We all wonder the same thing: What the hell is in this vaccine?

My sleep is broken, tossing between shallow dreams and the sharp thought: *Am I going to die?* Or worse, will my heart be permanently damaged? Dread sits heavy in my chest, matching the erratic rhythm of my pulse.

Morning comes, too bright and too soon. A nurse delivers a light breakfast: cereal and milk. No caffeine, apparently my heart has enough drama already.

Thankfully, I'm first in line for the heart stress test. Not that I'm remotely dressed for it. I left home halfway through getting ready for work, so I'm wearing whatever I'd thrown on in a panic. Let's just say there's no supportive sports bra in this situation, gravity is about to get a front-row seat.

The technician, a calm man with the steady tone of someone who's seen worse, explains the process: how the treadmill will speed up, what

they're measuring, and when I should speak up. Leads are stuck to my chest, cold against my skin, wires looping like vines. I step onto the treadmill, my bare shoulders prickling under the hospital air, and start walking. Slow at first, then brisk, then brisker still, fifteen minutes of mechanical pacing.

When it's over, the tech gives me the good news: everything looks great. Then the caveat, only a specialist can confirm the results. Back to my room I go, waiting again, that silent uncertainty filling the walls.

Then, at last, salvation. The morning tea trolley rolls by, metal wheels squeaking on linoleum. The smell of coffee hits me, and I practically leap for it. It's hospital-grade, burnt, thin, and utterly divine in this moment. I drink it as if it's a glass of champagne, each bitter gulp a tiny celebration of being alive, well, at least for now.

Soon enough, the results are in. Cleared of any heart stress. Interesting. No heart attack, no lasting damage, at least nothing they can measure, but still no explanation for why my body went into full revolt after the vaccine.

They discharge me with a single sheet of paper: *Reaction to Covid vaccine, reason unknown.* And that's it. Neat, vague, and utterly useless. A tidy way for a government-run hospital to cover its bases, acknowledge just enough without admitting anything.

I step outside into the glare of morning light, flag a taxi, and slide into the back seat. The ride home is short, the city rolling past in a blur of traffic and pure blue sky.

I'm told to rest for the next few days, so I call work and arrange the time off. Then I sit in my apartment, staring at the walls, wondering what the hell my next move should be. My brain, twisted, reckless, whispers, *Jane, drink like there's no tomorrow.*

And maybe there isn't.

So I do.

I rest up as ordered and it's now time to head off to Tasmania. Mum had just moved into her dream home, years in the making. After my stepfather passed away, fourteen years earlier, she'd talked about moving to Tassie. Slower pace. Cooler climate. A fresh start. Now, she's finally done it. A white weatherboard cottage, a majestic rose garden, fruit trees and clean, crisp air. I fly down to help her unpack, eager for a change of scenery, and maybe, to reset my own life a little too.

COVID restrictions are still hanging around, but things in Tasmania aren't as strict. At the airport, all I have to do is flash my ID and pass a temperature check. Masks were required on the plane and in the terminal, standard stuff by now, but no real hassle.

The moment I land, I'm struck by the cold, it wraps around me like a sharp breath of mountain air. Everything feels fresh and alive. Hills roll out like a green quilt stitched with trees, and the sky is so clear it feels like you can see right through it.

I fall in love with the place instantly.

We spend the first few days unpacking boxes and setting up Mum's new world. There's champagne every night, well, for me mostly. We take small road trips, exploring the coastline, dipping into towns with names that sound like secrets. Everywhere we go, there's this quiet beauty, mist on the hills, wildlife everywhere you look and winding roads to follow.

One night, wrapped in a blanket with a glass of bubbly in hand, Mum gently asks me about the drinking. About *him*. About everything. She doesn't scold. She listens. Offers advice like a soft nudge, not a lecture. She says she is concerned about my drinking, but she knows not to push that button too hard, the result will not be good. The worst thing you can say to an alcoholic is to tell them they are out of control. We know we are and to hear it, well, with me, it makes me want to drink more! A gentle nudge is the way to go…trust me!

I return to Brisbane, a little more relaxed but not sure what the hell I am doing…then an epiphany hits me like lightning through fog.

I realize I've felt most at ease, most "myself", with two men who were completely wrong for me. They shared the same dark traits, the same patterns. All they did was hurt me, and I *let* them.

That's the gut punch. I feel like I am walking around with - *I am a narcissist's dream come true* - tattooed to my forehead!

I see it now: if I don't stop drinking, I'm going to keep letting him back in. Keep letting *them* in. It's the booze that lowers the guardrails, that softens my resolve, that whispers maybe it wasn't *that* bad.

So I try to detox on my own. I tell myself I've only been drinking heavily again for six months, it can't be that hard, right?

But even as I say it, I know better.

I go to my doctor and ask for Diazepam, to help take the edge off when I stop. I know what's coming. The shakes. The anxiety. The racing heart at 3 a.m. when your body starts screaming for the thing you're trying to take away. I need something to soften the landing.

I choose a weekend when I'm already supposed to stop drinking. I'm prepping for a colonoscopy, which means no alcohol, no food, just clear fluids. In my head, it makes perfect sense. Two birds, one stone. I'll already be off the booze, seems like the perfect window to start.

Spoiler alert: it's not.

The prep is brutal on its own, those disgusting drinks that strip your insides, the endless trips to the bathroom, the hollow feeling that settles in your belly. And then, the procedure. I hadn't factored in the anesthesia. Or the fact that I was running on an empty stomach, weak, dehydrated, already chemically off-balance. After the colonoscopy, I crash—hard.

My body spirals. I get violently sick, heart pounding, skin clammy, vision flickering at the edges. At one point, I wonder if this is what it feels like to overdose. I'd mixed Diazepam, withdrawal, anesthesia, and starvation, and my body was screaming for help.

This wasn't detox. This was dangerous.

And it hits me: I can't do this alone. I've tried every shortcut. Every self-made plan. I've white-knuckled it, justified it, disguised it. But I'm out of rope now.

It's time to get help. **AGAIN!**

PART THREE
The Third Rehab

CHAPTER FOURTEEN

The Retreat

So, I come up with this brilliant idea: maybe what I need isn't just another rehab, but something more like a wellness retreat. Something that doesn't just focus on alcohol, but on the *why* behind it all. I'm looking for healing, not just sobriety.

The catch? My health insurance won't cover this kind of holistic treatment. Of course not. But I'm determined. So, I bite the bullet. I'll pay for it myself.

We're not talking pocket change here, these places range from $30,000 to over $100,000. The kind of money that makes your stomach clench. But at this point, I'm desperate for something that *works*. Because this isn't just about the drinking anymore. It's about how I let someone destroy me. How I believed the cruel things he said. How I made his words my truth.

I need to understand *why*. Why do I keep putting myself through this? What shaped me into the person who tolerates this kind of pain?

I dive into research on substance abuse and mental health retreats, comparing glossy websites and testimonials, weighing therapy hours against price tags. Eventually, I settle on one located in the Sunshine Coast Hinterland. It looks peaceful, quiet and is surrounded by rainforest.

The place offers a four-week program with everything: eighty hours of group therapy, eight hours one-on-one with a psychologist, daily yoga and personal training, massage therapy, art therapy, mindfulness sessions, nutrition education, a private chef, a magnesium pool, sauna, plunge pool, I choose the option of a shared villas with my own private bedroom and ensuite.

It sounds like the full reset I've been craving. And it's the most affordable of the bunch. *Relatively* speaking.

I access some of my Superannuation to cover the cost, because this feels like an investment in staying alive. My family and friends give their full support, hopeful this time will be *the* time.

I convince myself it's going to work. I mean, *how could it not?* I'm spending a ridiculous amount of money, committing to four weeks of intensive therapy, surrounded by professionals in paradise. I'm all in. Surely this will fix me.

October 2021, booking with the retreat, arranged. Time off work again, arranged. I am blessed to have such a supportive manager, I will be forever grateful to him for his care and understanding.

Bags packed, I climb into the same red Getz that carried me to my last rehab. My beloved flatmate is once again at the wheel, calm hands on the steering and soft music for our journey from the speakers. We pull out of the driveway and head toward what I hope will be my last shot at sobriety, and maybe something more.

By midmorning, we arrive. The property is tucked deep in the rainforest, just as I'd imagined: quiet, serene, and drenched in every shade of green, like something lifted straight from the tropics of North Queensland. I accept the offer from my flatmatemate to come in with me this time and we make our way to the main house to check in.

The heart of the retreat, the main house, is a sprawling farmhouse spread across a single level. Wide, open living rooms stretch out before us, anchored by an open stone fireplace that still carries the faint, smoky scent of a past night's fire. The kitchen feels like something out of a country bistro, its air warm with lingering traces of roasted garlic and fresh herbs, the tang of citrus cutting through as if someone has just sliced open a lemon. Long counters gleam under the light, pots hang overhead, and the space feels alive with the memory of meals cooked for a crowd.

Down the hallway, multiple rooms branch off, their doors slightly ajar. Outside, a massive stone deck opens to the rainforest air, damp earth and wild orchids mingling, while the glittering, resort-style pool sends up a cool, mineral freshness that shimmers even in the soft rainforest light.

One of the larger rooms has been converted into an office. We find a lovely woman there, warm smile ready, she's been expecting us. She welcomes us to the retreat, making me feel relaxed and confident I am in the right place.

I start the registration process, and I'm told I will have to hand over all my medication so it can be dispensed as needed. I am handed a water bottle with my name labeled on it, a pen and a note book. Then comes the hard part: surrendering my phone. They lock it away in a safe, no exceptions. From now on, all calls must be made from the "house phone", a good old-fashioned landline with a cord and everything. There will be no TV, no digital distractions. Just a well-stocked library, offering the kind of books you can lose yourself in, or maybe find yourself in.

Next, we're shown to my villa, set about a hundred meters from the main house, nestled among tall gum trees with a gentle stream running behind it. A few timber stairs lead up to a small deck that overlooks the water, the sound of it trickling over stones adding a soft, constant hush to the air. Glass sliding doors open into a shared common space: a table and chairs, a small lounge, and a modest kitchen setup with a bench, sink, microwave, and kettle.

Off to the right is my room and ensuite. It's a cute little space, simple and calming. There's a queen-size bed, a small cupboard to store my clothes, and not much else. But it's enough. It feels like a place I could settle into, maybe even exhale in.

My flatmate brings my luggage in from the car and we say our goodbyes, once again knowing I will see him soon. I unpack slowly, letting the stillness settle over me. Then I head back to the main house for a tour. This is where everything happens, group therapy, private sessions, yoga, meals. The kitchen smells amazing already, and I'm genuinely excited for the food. A private chef? Yes, please. For once, my body might actually be treated like something worth nourishing.

In the afternoon, I head into town with one of the lovely support workers for a doctor's visit. He's kind but thorough, going through my medical history and current medications. He also prescribes me a limited amount of Diazepam for my detox over the next two days. Then comes the inevitable: a full blood workup to assess what kind of havoc I may have wreaked on my body once again.

Back at the retreat it's now 4:00 p.m. and we're ushered into our first "group therapy" session, mandatory, this will occur every single day. I've never done anything like this before and have no idea what to expect. One of the retreat therapists leads the session; they'll be rotating in and out over the coming days.

We all take seats in a loose circle, the kind that makes you feel both exposed and held at the same time. The room smells faintly of sandalwood, and there's a quiet hum of nerves and anticipation in the air. We begin with individual check-ins, going around the circle one by one. Each person shares how they're feeling and whether anything in particular is weighing on them that day.

Listening to everyone crack open their inner world, some tentative, others pouring out, feels oddly comforting. There's something strangely therapeutic about hearing we're all here for the same messy, chaotic, beautiful reasons. In this moment, I don't feel so different. I feel... normal.

Dinner is at 6:30 in the main house. We gather around a long, rustic wooden table that feels like it belongs in a movie, warm lighting, mismatched chairs, and the buzz of conversation. It's got that "found family" vibe, and I love it. The food is next-level, pure, organic, no preservatives, no salt, no sugar. Every plate is tailored to the portion size we've chosen. It is here I find out there is NO CAFFINE, what NO COFFEE OR TEA!!! Only herbal tea, no sugar either. This will be interesting.

Then comes dessert. All natural, no added sugar, just genius. Tonight, it's chocolate mousse, smooth and rich, and shockingly made from avocado and cacao. The chef has absolutely outdone herself. If someone hadn't told me, I would never have guessed.

After dinner, we shift into the lounge for a mindfulness session. Some of us stretch out on the floor, others curl into armchairs. The space is dim, serene, and smells faintly of essential oils. One of the support workers guides us through a twenty minute exercise. Her voice is soft, steady. I try to focus, to be present, but my mind keeps darting off like a kid on too much sugar. Still, I get it, that's part of the work. I'll get better.

Afterward, we're free to hang out in the house, read, play board games, do puzzles, or wander back to our villas to wind down for the night.

This is the rhythm I'll be living for the next four weeks. And honestly? I'm okay with that. I feel a sense of calm settling into my bones. Progress is happening.

Day Two dawns misty and cool, the valley wrapped in a soft grey hush. Birdsong threads through the trees, a kind of morning lullaby. I pull on my workout gear for the pre-breakfast exercise session. Today, it's boxing.

It's wild fun and totally exhausting. The trainer has us sweating within minutes, jabbing at pads, ducking imaginary punches, moving like we're in a real ring. I feel every muscle wake up and scream in protest, but in the best possible way.

Breakfast is another kind of knockout. A beautiful spread greets me with the buttery scent of eggs sizzling on the griddle, mingling with the nutty, toasty fragrance of homemade muesli that crunches just right Coconut yogurt, no dairy allowed here, alongside fresh fruit and thick-cut sourdough toast. I make myself a cup of herbal tea and, surprise, I actually find one I like. Rooibos. Warm, earthy and a little sweet.

I head to my first appointment with the psychologist they've matched me with. She greets me with a calm smile and introduces herself as a forensic psychologist.

Forensic? I blink. *What am I, a crime scene?*

I don't say that out loud, but the thought crosses my mind. I'm here for alcohol addiction, why would I need someone trained in criminal profiling?

Still, I sit down, give her a chance, and start talking. I explain why I'm here, what's led me back to this point. When she asks whether I want to cut down or completely abstain from alcohol, I nearly fall off the couch.

Cut down? I'm horrified. I've forked out a small fortune to *quit,* not moderate.

Once we're clear on that, things shift. We're on the same page, well I think so. I decide to trust her. She listens deeply, no judgment, no sugarcoating, just quiet, informed, and presence. I can feel her holding the space for me to unpack everything, even the parts I usually keep zipped up tight. I can't wait to hear her views on my last mistake, we will unpack *him* in the next session.

Lunch is another masterclass in how to eat clean and well. Vibrant colours on the plate, flavors that don't need salt to sing. If this is what healthy tastes like, I could absolutely get used to it. After our feast, the psychologists take turns leading sessions designed to deepen our understanding of how alcohol affects the brain and body. They also walk us through practical coping mechanisms for managing cravings. Most of it, I've heard before, but hearing it again isn't a bad thing. Sooner or later, it has to stick.

Later that day, I have massage therapy, and honestly? It's heaven. Warm oil, strong hands, and sixty minutes where I don't have to think or explain myself. It ends up being one of the highlights of the entire program, something that reminds me I deserve to be looked after.

The nightly rhythm settles in like a familiar lullaby, family-style dinner around the big table, a calming mindfulness session, quiet chats in the lounge as we all get to know each other a little better. Then it's off to bed, where the forest chirps and whispers outside my villa, lulling me to sleep.

Three days in, and it's time for my first personal training session. Oh boy. This should be interesting. I don't "do" exercise, unless you count walking, and that's about as intense as I get. But here I am, standing in the retreat's gym, trying to look like I belong while bracing for pain.

Surprisingly, it's not awful. The trainer is kind, realistic. He builds a weight program tailored to my non-existent fitness level and my old back injury. No bootcamp madness, just steady, doable moves to build strength and endurance. Apparently, this is now a daily thing: lower-body focus one day, upper the next. The hour slips by faster than I expect, and I leave feeling sore, but also kind of proud. Maybe I'll even lose a bit of weight along the way. Who knows?

I have the afternoon to myself, so I explore. The sauna, radiant with heat, earthy and dry. The magnesium pool shimmers invitingly, and the main pool sparkles under a sky that's finally burned off the morning mist. I try each one like a kid with a whole amusement park to herself.

Later, I stretch out on a sun lounge, a book in hand, the warmth of the day sinking deep into my skin. All too soon, it's time to pack up, and head into the group therapy session, it is another enlightening afternoon.

The next day is my scheduled appointment with the forensic psychologist for our second session, closing out my first week here. Today's the hard stuff. Not just the alcohol, but *him*. The man who dragged me back down to my lowest self, again.

I start telling her about the awful things he used to say, the texts, the name calling. She nods, calm and clinical, then asks me to grab my phone from the safe. "Let's see if your little keyboard warrior has left any surprises," she says lightly.

I power on the phone, and it *blows up*. Pings, alerts, message after message. *Oh god*. My stomach drops.

True to form, the messages are vile. Name-calling, insults, all the usual poison. Then it escalates, he claims he's watching me. Which is odd, considering I'm *not even home*. Then we read the worst one: a warning to watch my car because it might be set on fire. (He admitted to me had set fire to his former partners car in anger)

The psychologist goes quiet for a moment, then says, "Jane, he's borderline dysphoric. (this is a mixture of intense emotions like anger, identity loss, victimisation and a lack of control). You need to be careful."

Oh no.

We talk it through. She gently, but firmly, urges me to consider a protection order, not just for me, but for my family. I don't like the sound of it, but deep down, I know she's right. After the session I arrange an appointment with the local police station to go in and make a report to apply for the order.

CHAPTER FIFTEEN

The Break Through

The first weekend arrives, and for the most part, it's business as usual, morning exercise, then breakfast. But here's a curveball: no chef on the weekends. They return for Sunday dinner, and until then, we're on our own. A spread of ingredients is laid out for us like a DIY buffet, and we fend for ourselves. Also, that night is a BBQ dinner . We cook that ourselves too, this will be interesting. Nothing says team bonding like standing around a fire and burning steaks.

Saturday brings a different energy. It's group therapy day, but with a twist. The focus is solely on our mental health, to deal with what we're still carrying from childhood or struggling with in our present lives. The therapist leads us through roleplays, using us, the clients, as stand-ins for each other's family members. It's intense, raw and confronting. Standing in someone else's emotional shoes, helping them unpack their pain, is no small thing.

Today, it's not my turn to lay out my past. I watch. I listen. I learn. But there's no guarantee I'll be chosen next time. These sessions don't follow a script, anything can happen in the weeks ahead.

Sunday is even better, it's family visit day! My son, daughter-in-law, grandson, and granddaughter arrive to join me for lunch and a relaxed afternoon together. We share sandwiches I've made with treats from the kitchen, then I take them on a tour of my villa and the lush rainforest that surrounds it. We finish the visit with a hot sauna followed by a bracing swim with the grandkids. I'm over the moon to see them and deeply grateful they still stand by me after everything. The love I have for them surpasses anything else in my life.

The time comes to say goodbye. It's bittersweet, my chest tightens, but I remind myself it's not forever. I'll see them again soon. Their faces glow with quiet pride, and I can tell they see the change in me. I'm standing straighter, feeling lighter, the softness around my jaw giving way to sharper lines. There's colour in my cheeks again.

Then my son turns to me, his eyes steady, voice low but clear. "Mum, if you ever pick up a drink again, it'll be a $30,000 drink."

The words land like a punch to the ribs, sudden, true, and unforgettable.

He's right. And I know, deep in my bones, I'll never forget that.

The first week is done, and I'm handling it a hell of a lot better than I did in my last two stints. This place, this experience, is different. It's not the sterile, hospital-style rehab I've known before. There's more freedom, more humanity.

I meet some amazing people at the retreat. Mental health issues and addiction don't discriminate, we're an eclectic mix, and that's putting it mildly. Here, things are different. We're allowed to exchange contact details if we want to. There's me, a supply chain professional with alcohol dependency and mental health issues I haven't even begun to unpack. Then there's a heart surgeon, a politician, a musician, a finance professional, a cowboy, and a few homemakers. People come and go at different times during my stay, each carrying their own weight, their own stories.

One day, a lovely young woman arrives in a whirlwind, flustered, lost, unsure if she's in the right place. She becomes a dear friend and confidante, even now. It's her turn to introduce herself, and she speaks a mile a minute, barely pausing to breathe. The therapist gently interrupts and tells her to slow down. "You sound like you're talking underwater," he says. We all burst into laughter, and just like that, the tension breaks. She relaxes. She's one of us now, part of our strange, healing little family.

The day comes when I must go to the police station to apply for a protection order against *him*. It's overwhelming. I have to recount everything, what he said, what he threatened, and show the texts to back it all up. My voice shakes, but I get through it. The paperwork will now go to the local court, where a judge will set a hearing and decide whether to grant the order, and for how long. I'm asking for five years.

While I'm in town with a support worker, we duck into the chemist and the supermarket to pick up things for the others back at the retreat, magazines, sugar-free lollies, cigarettes, toiletries. I seize the chance for a brief taste of freedom and sneak into a café for a real coffee. A proper, fair dinkum coffee. Ohhhhh, heaven. Do I feel guilty? Not for a second.

Art therapy day arrives, and I'm buzzing with anticipation. I love arts and crafts. The room is set up like an artist's dream: blank full-face masks laid out on the table, surrounded by tubes of paint, feathers, rhinestones, glitter, glue, felt pens, and brushes. Today's exercise is about the masks we all wear, what we show the world versus what we truly feel inside.

I throw myself into it. The outside of my mask is a riot of colour, hot pinks, electric blues, sunshine yellows, and bright purples. I glue feathers and glitter along the edges, making it as joyful and loud as I can. But the inside tells another story. I paint in deep blacks, angry reds, olive greens, fractured, messy and raw. That's the truth of it, that's me, on the inside, just barely holding it together. As a functioning alcoholic, the face I show the world is one of pure happiness and control, but this is hiding the fact I am far from this facade I present.

A close second favourite activity are the therapeutic massage sessions. There are three massage therapists, each with their own unique style. I adore the one we call the "hippie lady." She's so free-spirited, so earthy. She even massages my bum, there's no awkwardness, just easy comfort. It's the most relaxed I've felt in years.

But even so, I'm starting to notice the cracks, literally and figuratively. The building shows its age, equipment breaks down frequently, the magnesium pool closed for two of my four week stay for an unexplained problem, and the main oven in the kitchen is out of service for a week. For the price we're all paying to be here, you'd expect the place to feel a little more put together. A little less like it's barely holding on.

The days slip into weeks, and my mental health is improving steadily. The drinking? That's another story. My sessions with the psychologist are mostly good. She introduces me to a few apps, calming music, bedtime stories, guided meditations. I test some out while I have my phone, and I know I'll use them when I'm back home.

During these sessions, we also check for messages from *him*. There are many. They're not getting better. She tells me not to reply. He doesn't know where I am, and we're keeping it that way.

My final Saturday arrives, therapy day and the room is alive with energy. Our group role-play session is in full swing, laughter, tears, breakthroughs. Therapy in motion. Then, it's my turn.

Oh God. Here we go. This should be interesting.

I already know what's coming, more or less. But how will I respond? That's the part I can't predict. During my private sessions, my psychologist suggested that if I get called up to work through something, I should focus on my childhood.

It always comes back to abandonment.

From as early as I can remember, my Mum was leaving, leaving the house, leaving my dad, and by extension, leaving me and my older brother (four years my senior). She'd decide to leave without warning, we never understood why, sometimes she took us with her, or we would be left, Just two kids blinking in the silence, wondering what we'd done wrong. Then she would come back, and unbelievably my dad would always accept her with loving arms.

Then that time came, I was just eleven years old, and she just ran away with another man. Ran all the way to Perth, Western Australia. My brother and I were devastated. She said goodbye and that was that. Now it is just dad, me and my brother. I am the mother of the house, lots of burnt steaks and canned food coming up for dinner. It was fifteen months before she came back, with her new man and my dad had also moved on with a new lady, two fractured families.

That's where the damage started. What I have learnt in my sessions is I still carry it.

So now, whenever someone shows me a sliver of affection, I cling to them like my life depends on it. Even when I know they're bad for me. Even when I know they'll hurt me. I just don't want to be abandoned again.

The facilitator calls me forward. Her voice is gentle but firm. "What is it you want to let go of today? What trauma are you ready to face?"

I don't hesitate. "I want to stop feeling the pain of my Mum leaving. Of always being left behind."

She looks at me—really looks—and says without missing a beat, "You need to forgive your mother."

The words hit me in the chest.

"You'll probably never know why she did what she did," she continues. "But she did it. And you're still carrying the anger, the grief, the weight of it all. You have to let it out. You have to forgive her."

She asks me to choose someone from our group to play the role of my mother. I hesitate for a moment, scan the circle, then point to my new friend, the lovely lady who can talk underwater. The session begins.

Next, she tells me to go outside and find a large rock from the garden. A rock?

I blink at her, caught off guard by the odd request. But I nod and walk out into the garden, I crouch beside a bush and search until I find one that feels right, rough, solid, heavy. I pick it up with both hands, its weight grounding, slightly cold against my palms.

Back inside, she tells me to hand it to the person standing in as my mother. I do.

"Now," she says, "tell her what you're angry about."

The words tumble up before I can stop them. "I'm angry that you left home so many times, leaving my father to clean up the mess."

"Put it into that rock," the therapist says.

"How?" I ask, genuinely confused.

"Yell at it," she says. "Get that anger out of you and into the rock."

So I do.

At first, I feel ridiculous, shouting at a rock. But then something clicks. My voice rises. I yell about the absences, the broken promises, the way it all piled up. I pour it out, every jagged memory, every raw edge. My hands tremble, my throat stings, and still I yell until there's nothing left.

Then she tells me to take the rock back outside and throw it into the garden, hard.

I walk out again, the rock cradled in my arms like something sacred and volatile. I draw my arms up in the air and throw it down with everything I have. It lands with a dull thud in the soil.

That's it. That's the moment.

I feel it instantly. Lighter. Emptied in the best possible way. Like I've made space inside myself that anger no longer occupies. I'm not carrying it anymore, and I won't let it come back.

The rest of Saturday drifts by in a haze of warmth and stillness. I stretch out beside the pool, soaking up the spring sun. Every now and then, I slip into the water, letting it cradle me. I float on my back, eyes closed, the surface cool against my skin. There's no tightness in my body, no weight dragging at my thoughts. Just light. Just quiet.

It's now my last week here and I am looking forward to going home, going back to a better life now that I understand a lot more about myself. I have my final session with the psychologist and I want to focus on my alcohol problem. She says something that hits me sideways: "You're doing well, you'll even be able to have a glass of champagne with your Christmas lunch."

What the fuck?

I stare at her, stunned. Why would she say that? I remind her, again, that I'm here because I have a problem. If I start drinking, I *can't stop*. That's the whole point. In that moment, I lose all trust in her. This sets a seed in my mind that should have NEVER been planted by a professional!

Later in that week I learn from the local police that a temporary protection order has been granted against *him*. The case is scheduled to be heard by a magistrate on the Sunshine Coast in November 2021. I'll be required to attend.

With the final massages completed, I pack my bags and prepare to farewell the retreat, and the people I now call friends. My ride home pulls into the driveway: my amazing flatmate is behind the wheel of his trusty red Getz. I climb in, close the door, and settle in for the scenic drive back to our apartment. Lets hope I have learnt something this time….

CHAPTER SIXTEEN

Life After the Third Rehab – Sobriety Take Three

Back in Brisbane. Back to work. Back to my routine. This time, I'm focused, no distractions, no bad men cluttering up my life. That's the plan, anyway.

October slides into November, I have to attend court up the Sunshine Coast, the hearing for the protection order against *him*. My stomach twists; I don't want to see him.

The courthouse looms ahead, a big, imposing brick monolith that seems to swallow the light. I climb the wide concrete stairs, the echo of my footsteps loud in the morning air, and step inside. The reception area smells faintly of disinfectant and old paper. I wait in line, every tick of the clock scraping against my nerves.

When my turn comes, they take my name and direct me to the victim waiting area at the far end of the building. I pass the heavy wooden doors to the court chambers, the brass handles gleaming in the dim light, and slip through one room with rattling concertina doors into another space lined with a couple of worn lounges and scattered chairs.

There are quite a few people here, some flanked by lawyers who murmur in low, practiced tones. I sink into a seat, my insides churning. How the hell did it come to this? Why did I ever let him into my life?

An hour crawls by before I finally need to use the ladies' room. I ask where it is and am told it's near the front of the building.

I head back out, pushing through the other room, and freeze. *He's* there. Sitting in a chair. Staring right at me.

What the hell? To reach the bathroom, victims have to walk past the accused? The air turns metallic in my mouth, my skin prickling. Oh God. I swallow hard, force my eyes straight ahead, and keep walking. My pulse hammers. Shit. I'm shaking like a leaf, but I make it to the toilets and shut myself inside, pressing my palms against the cool sink until my breath comes back.

When I leave, I lift my chin, fix my gaze forward, and walk past as if I don't see him. I will not let him affect me anymore.

Back in the waiting area, a court support worker approaches. She explains I'll be called soon, tells where to sit, what to say to the judge, and that *he'll* be on the other side of the room. I won't have to acknowledge or even look at him. Relief seeps through.

Finally, my case is called. My legs feel heavy as I step into the courtroom. I walk down the right-hand side of the aisle, moving toward the front where two uniformed police officers stand, I slide into place beside them, their presence reassuring. The judge is already in her seat. Her voice is firm but measured as she asks us all to sit. The air feels thick, every sound amplified, the shuffle of papers, the faint hum of the overhead lights.

The case unfolds quickly. His plea is taken - "guilty". Then, in a voice that carries the weight of finality, the judge grants a five-year protection order. *He* is not to come near me or my family, not to contact me, in any way, for the entire duration.

Relief floods me, sharp and clean, like stepping out into fresh air after a storm. This is a good outcome. I can go home. I can start living my life again.

One blink, and it's December. I'm doing well. I know the drill this time. I'm tired, yes, and I sleep a lot, but instead of fighting it, I fold it into my routine. I refuse to fall into that old trap of pouring a drink just to jolt some energy into my veins.

Today, my BMW needs new front tyres and her annual service, so I drive down to the local service centre. I decide to wait in the lounge, treating myself to a perfectly smooth cup of coffee. The rich, roasted aroma clings to my senses as I wander into the showroom, where the convertibles gleam under the lights like jewels under glass. Oh, they are divine. I run my hand over a door handle, imagining the purr of the engine beneath me, Iv'e always wanted a convertible, if only I could afford one.

Well, Jane, why not take a peek at the pre-loved lot next door?

I step outside, the sun warm on my shoulders, and there she is, my car. Or at least, I hope so. Sleek, polished even in her unwashed state, gunmetal grey in colour, she waits for me like we've known each other forever. I open the door. The scent of leather greets me, rich and buttery. Beige leather seats cradle the interior, woodgrain glows on the dash and door panels, trimmed in black and silver. She fits me like a bespoke suit.

I all but jog to find a salesperson. It's early, just after nine, and they're barely starting their day. I tell him I would like to test drive the convertible. He explains it only arrived yesterday and hasn't even been cleaned yet, I might want to come back.

"Oh no," I say. "That doesn't matter. I'd like to take her for a spin now. My car's being serviced next door."

Keys in hand, he takes my details for insurance, runs me through the controls, exactly the same as my 328i sedan, only smaller, sportier. This one is a 228i. He shows me how to drop the roof, and I'm gone.

Truth is, I've already bought her in my mind. The drive is just a formality. I ease through city streets, slipping out into the suburbs. I can't push her too hard, but I can feel her potential, I do test out that all-important sports mode. Roof down, wind whipping my hair into a glorious mess, music blasting so the bass thrums in my chest, yes, she's mine.

I pull into a local park, sunlight flashing off her curves, and take a few selfies. I send one to my son with a cheeky caption about my new ride. I feel giddy, like I've just fallen in love, and maybe I have. This isn't just a car. It's a new chapter.

Back at the yard, I find the salesperson and tell him flat out: I'll take her. She'll need cleaning and detailing, which means I can't pick her up for a week. Fine by me. We arrange the trade-in appraisal and a quick meeting with finance.

An hour later, the deal is done. I've just bought my second BMW. And I can already hear the open road calling my name.

The day finally arrives, I can pick up my new car. It's a Friday, perfect for a whole weekend of driving. I slide into the driver's seat, the new-leather scent wrapping around me. The steering wheel feels cool and smooth beneath my fingers. She's mine.

I pull into my family's driveway, eager to show her off. The grandkids spill out onto the lawn, their eyes wide, mouths open. I press the button, the roof folds down with a mechanical purr.

"What!" they shout, jumping up and down. Laughter spills out of me.

It's only a week until Christmas. The streets are strung with lights, the air tinged with excitement, tinsel everywhere, and I love it. I'm looking forward to this one.

Until—my phone buzzes. A text. From *him*.

Oh crap. I forgot to block his number after the court case.

He's not supposed to be contacting me. I have a protection order. My stomach knots. The message is short, almost harmless: *Merry Christmas*.

But that's all it takes to tilt my world off its axis.

Why does hearing from him awaken feelings I thought were buried? I'm confused, angry at myself. I don't want to feel this way. I can't.

What the hell is wrong with me?

I still have two unused follow-up sessions with the psychologist from the retreat, so I book a Zoom call with her. When her face appears on the screen, I tell her how I've been doing, and then I confess the problem. He texted me, and now all these stupid, tangled feelings have bubbled to the surface.

She listens, her expression warm and steady, and says I'm feeling sad for him because of what happened, that part of me still carries guilt over the fallout. I lean back in my chair, frowning. *Hmm.* That doesn't help much.

I shift the conversation to something brighter, my new car, my pride and joy. Her smile widens, and she suggests I join the BMW club.

"They have a club?" I ask, eyebrows lifting.

Now *that* is a great idea. As soon as the call ends, I head straight to google, the excitement buzzing in my chest as I start searching. It doesn't take long and I'm officially a member of the BMW Car Club Queensland. Their website is full of glossy photos: winding coastal drives, polished bonnets gleaming under the sun, smiling faces at weekend events. This looks like fun. I can almost feel the wind in my hair already.

Christmas Eve arrives. I duck into the liquor barn next to my apartment building, looking for something non-alcoholic to take to lunch tomorrow for the table. The cool air inside smells faintly of cork and fermented fruit. My eyes skim the shelves until they land on my favourite champagne, the foil glinting under the fluorescent lights.

And then I think something really stupid.

The psychologist said I could *probably* have a drink for Christmas. My alcoholic brain seizes on that, twisting it into permission. *See? It's fine.* My hand moves almost before I realize it, lifting the bottle and placing it in my trolley.

I tell myself I'll drink it tomorrow night, alone at home. No one needs to know. My flatmate's going away for a couple of months, no witnesses, no judgment. This will be fine.

I spend Christmas Day with my family, and it's wonderful. The mountain of presents under the tree shrinks to nothing but shredded paper carpeting the floor. The grandchildren zoom around in a frenzy, testing their new toys with shrieks of delight. In the kitchen, the air is heavy with the scent of roast ham and a special glaze. Punch sits in large glass jugs, one spiked with alcohol, one without, glittering in the light. I keep my hands busy, setting the long table for the lunchtime feast, lining up plates, smoothing napkins, making sure every seat is ready.

The celebrations wind down in a happy exhaustion. We're all stuffed and content. I leave them in the warm chaos of a day well done and head out, driving home to pick up my flatmate. I drop him at the airport, wave him off to his holiday.

And then, I'm home. Alone for the next two months.

Christmas night. The streets outside are quiet, the faint twinkle of lights in windows a reminder of other people's evenings. In my fridge, that bottle of champagne waits for me, icy cold, condensation misting on its dark green glass. It feels like it has my name etched on it.

I take my old faithful flute from the cupboard. Grab that bottle and pop the cork with a sharp crack that echoes in the empty apartment. *I'll only have one glass,* I tell myself. I pour, the fizz racing to the top, and convince myself I deserve this. Just one. That will be it. (*How fucking delusional I am.*)

I drink the bottle. All of it. The taste isn't even what I remember, It tastes like guilt more than anything else. That was a $30,000 drink!! Just as my son had warned me.

I decide I won't tell anyone. I'm not going to do it again…surely.

A few days later, my phone pings. Another text.

It's *him*.

I did nothing wrong, it says.

Are you kidding me? My stomach twists. Anger flares, but under it, God help me, I feel sorry for him. I can almost hear his voice, low and coaxing, the one that used to make me feel like I was the only person in the world. *Oh, Jane. Don't feel like this.*

CHAPTER SEVENTEEN
Will I Ever learn?

It's December 31, 2021. I sit on the lounge with a fresh notebook, the crisp pages smelling faintly of paper and promise, and I write my 2022 goals:
- Forget the bad relationship of 2021
- Stay sober
- Get active
- Get social

January 1, 2022, I write again, neat and firm: *This is the year to move on and forget 2021. Don't look back.*

Wise words. But I don't listen. The truth is, I still feel brokenhearted. The days pass in a blur. I'm fighting a stubborn sinus infection, my body heavy and drained. Loneliness creeps in, quiet and relentless, settling into my bones.

He texts again. He wants to talk, he has a proposition.

And then I do what only Jane could be foolish enough to do.

I let him back in.

I agree to talk to him .

Even as I type the words, I feel that small, dangerous flicker, remembering how it felt to be wanted by him.

Oh. No.

He tells me he's changed. He's learnt his lesson. He admits he treated me terribly and swears he'd never do it again. He says he just wants to be friends, to enjoy each other's company with no pressure.

I still feel this pull toward him, this gnawing need to see him, to help him. Why? I have no fucking idea. There's a protection order hanging over this whole mess, and here I am, thinking this could be ok.

I tell myself it's my choice. My decision.

And then, of course, I agree to see him. But not without setting some ground rules, at least, that's the plan. I even sit down and make a list of pros and cons. Reading it back now, it's almost laughable. Here's one gem from the cons column: *How can he love me and still call me a lying c**t in the same breath?* And from the pros: *love and companionship*. The pattern is obvious, my craving to feel wanted outweighs everything else. And in the very next instant, I make what will become the next colossal mistake of my seriously fucked-up life.

He wants to be just friends, no pressure. For the next few weeks, we slip into a rhythm: meetups, daily texts and calls. To me, things are progressing way too fast. The time comes I must tell my family what I am doing. Oh boy. The look on their faces could strip paint off a wall. They're furious, beyond furious, that I'd be so stupid. Of course they're right, but stubbornness is my middle name. I'm not listening. Even as hairline cracks start forming in our so-called friendship.

Late February, in the middle of this emotional mess, I decide to move out of the city, closer to my family and work. My flatmate's ready to move on too, which feels like a blessing in disguise. I start hunting for units and townhouses, and then, there it is. A place in the exact complex I've been eyeing for ages. My bestie lives there. It's perfect: ten minutes to my son and his family's place, ten minutes to work. I don't hesitate. I inspect it, apply on the spot. The rent's higher than what I'm paying now, but it's worth it to put some distance between me and temptation.

I am successful with my application and I'm moving in the first week of April. The boxes start piling up, connection dates get set. Things with *him* keep spiraling, but I keep thinking maybe, just maybe, living closer to everyone will fix it. It doesn't.

The next month is a tug-of-war: fights, cold silences, blocked numbers, unblocked numbers, then the inevitable happens. He pushes the nastiness over the line. I am furious and I do something bad, very bad. Its Friday afternoon, I swing by the bottle shop and grab two bottles of my go-to champagne. I'm crashing at my bestie's place until I move, so I take them back, crack them open, and drink both. She doesn't say much, but I can see the concern in her eyes, like she's watching me inch toward a cliff.

Saturday morning hits like a freight train. My head pounds, my mouth tastes like I've been chewing on carpet, and sunlight feels personal. NOOO. This is the last thing I want. My bestie pokes her head in, eyes scanning me like she's taking a mental snapshot for the "before" picture. I burst into tears.

"He's fucked me up again," I sob, spilling the whole story. She does what she does best, just listens. When I run out of words, she tilts her head, soft but firm. "You're crazy to put up with it." That's all she says. I know she's right. I've always known.

I talked to *him* again a few days later, but I'm not forgiving, not forgetting.

Moving day arrives. I've had some things in storage, the overflow tucked away at his place. My delivery box comes in the morning, and later he shows up with the furniture stored there. We lug it all up, two flights of stairs, every step echoing with the reminder that I did this to myself. He crashes on the couch that night.

The next day, he drops his latest bomb: he's lost his job. For his own stupid reasons. I head off to work and by the time I get home, he's spent the entire day drinking. No job hunting, no plans, just booze. Nope.

I'm not doing this. We argue, and finally, I *really* see *him*. The man everyone else warned me about. The man I didn't want to admit he was.

He sleeps on the couch again and then next morning, I tell him to leave. Not just for the night, forever. I go to work, instructing him to leave the spare key on the stairs and be gone before I'm back. When I return, the key is there, the space empty. Relief floods me. New place. Clean slate. Fresh start. Sounds easy. Right?

Of course it isn't.

The texts start. Then the calls. Threatening, ugly and I start recording them. When it gets too much, I involve the law. I already have a protection order, and now I'm going to use it. I call Police Link, and they connect me to the domestic violence unit. I tell them everything. They send two officers to my door. I play the recordings. Show the texts. They nod, serious, and tell me to keep safe, to report to the local station in the morning so my statement can be taken. Not ideal, but it's the process. I block him, again.

The next morning, I walk into the station and brace myself for the humiliation of admitting I let him back in my life when there is a protection order involved. I'm mortified. But I do it. The officer taking my statement is professional, almost gentle. "This happens more than you'd think," he says. Comforting in a way, though it means there are a lot of us making bad choices.

When it's done, he explains the file will sit in a queue, don't expect quick action. The system's overloaded. He advises me to block all contact, watch my surroundings, take extra precautions, install security cameras if I don't already have them.

WOW. My own fault, my own mess so I will take care of things. I change my phone number, inconvenient but now necessary.

I settle into my new place like I've been here forever. I've bought a security camera for the front door, and linked it to my phone. Now

I can keep an eye on every knock, every shadow, every suspicious pair of sneakers.

For a while, everything's calm. Then the emails start. Oh, fantastic, he's found a way around me changing my number. And oh boy, they're *nasty*. Each subject line feels like a little slap before I even open it. I am losing my shit here.

Four weeks after moving in, I head down to Tassie. I need a break from this mess I built with my own two hands. Mum's there, and she's my safe harbor.

The trip is bliss. We explore the East Coast, chasing strips of white sand that look like postcards come to life. We bounce down random dirt roads just to see where they lead, end up at the northeastern tip of Tassie through a speck-on-the-map place called Little Musselroe Bay. The air smells like salt and eucalyptus, the kind of clean you can't bottle. And yes, I'm drinking again. Not much, not by my standards, but enough that it's slinking back in.

The visit's over too soon. I now face the abundance of emails. Even blocked, they still slither into my spam folder. And of course, I read them all. He's bold enough to ask me for money. *Money*. WTF. At this point, I'm convinced he's got serious mental health issues. I suspected it all along, but I thought foolishly that I could help.

I call the police station to check on my complaint. The officer tells me he's been charged and is due in court in late June. Finally, some good news. Maybe, just maybe, he'll get fined, or better yet, learn something that sticks.

Personally, I'm not doing well. Guilt clings like a damp jumper, heavy and hard to peel off. I know I shouldn't feel responsible for any of this, but knowing doesn't stop feeling.

I call the retreat I went to last year. I still have one follow-up session with a psychologist. The woman I saw before has moved on, a small blessing in disguise. So I make an appointment with another person. Fresh eyes. No history.

On June 10th, I drive into the hinterland, the road curling through rainforest and sunlight, the air cooler, and cleaner. I'm looking for answers again. My new psychologist is someone I'd seen around the retreat but never spoken to much. He greets me warmly, no judgment in his face, just space. I spill everything, how I let *him* back in, even with a protection order in place.

"Not uncommon," he says. I am relieved once again. "A lot of women take their partners back even when they have police enforced orders against them".

Finally, someone explains it so I understand these abandonment issues. Why I keep clutching at people who only ever offer crumbs? I grip onto anyone who shows me I might be lovable, even if loving me benefits them more than me. The fear of rejection drowns out all the sirens in my head. Logic gets steamrolled, gut instinct gets shoved in the corner. My alcoholic brain is also adding to the chaos.

From here on, I choose to act from my decision-making brain, the calm, clear center I've been ignoring. I listen to my instincts; they've been shouting the truth from day one.

The psychologist's words make me feel hopeful, his behavior has nothing to do with me. His cruelty, his silence, his reckless choices, they're his. I'm not responsible. I don't carry that guilt anymore. I shrug it off like an old coat that doesn't fit.

I choose now. I choose me.

No more relationships. No more numbing. It's time to get busy living, and maybe, just maybe, drink a little less. (Again.)

He also tells me the best analogy I have ever heard;

Learn to swim—When you are struggling, feeling vulnerable, DON'T grab onto the first thing that floats past—it's a log covered with barbed wire, let it float past—it is BAD for you. DON'T grab on to the next thing, it's soft and floaty, it's in another disguise, it's poo, no good for you either. The next thing to float past is a blow up raft, it's stable and will keep you afloat, gently grab a hold of it and let it help you get to safety.

The drinking has to stop. I know it now, down to the marrow, in every cell vibrating with the truth of it. My fingers hover over the keyboard, then fly: *how to stop drinking at home, quitting alcohol support.*

The web blooms open, a chaotic bazaar of programs, advice and books to read. I don't know where to start, but one name surfaces again and again, bobbing in the current: an online Recovery. I go to the website and see what it is all about. They are run by a trained facilitator for supporting any addictive behaviour, run weekly and free.

On June 20, I sign into my first Recovery Zoom meeting. My camera stays off, my mic mostly muted. I'm a shadow in the corner of the room, just listening. And yet, there's a pulse here, a steady buzz of possibility. The facilitator mentions a 10-day plan: prep your mindset, dodge your triggers, lower your stress. I seize the words like rope tossed into deep water - sign me up!

I circle Monday, June 27, in red ink to start the ten day plan. That's it. My new day one. The weekend becomes a soft training ground: eating clean, stretching my legs on long walks, scribbling into my journal, clearing cobwebs in my mind.

Then Monday comes, quiet as a storm gathering offshore. By 4:30 p.m., the pressure hits. The air feels tight, my skin prickles and my chest cinches. I can't. Not today. I cave. The shame is swift and sharp, but I don't let it drag me under. Instead, I grab the phone and schedule a doctor's call for tomorrow. Enough of the solo act.

The next day, right on time, the phone buzzes. It's the surgery, there's a locum filling in for my Doctor today. That's fine I tell them, I just need a prescription. I tell him my plan, my need for Diazepam to help manage any withdrawal symptoms. I want off this spinning ride, but cold turkey will break me. That night, I tell my family. I need them to know, to hold me steady. They do, gentle hands, worried eyes.

The new quit date arrives, bringing panic in its purest form. My thoughts whip into a cyclone. My hands tremble. My breath comes in shallow bursts. I'm not ready. I download a self-help book, hoping the words will stitch me together, or at least pull my mind somewhere else. I read, I breathe, I wait.

Tomorrow, I tell myself. Then again the next day. And the next. Each postponement is a small funeral, wrapped in the heavy cloth of self-loathing. I keep whispering that it's part of the process, even as the truth burns in my gut: I'm still standing at the edge.

CHAPTER EIGHTEEN

I Become a Race Car Driver at Age Fifty Six!

I am taking a step back, taking the pressure off and trying something new. I have registered for an afternoon skid pan session at the Mount Cotton Driver Training Centre where I will get to throw my car around a track to purposely lose control, putting her into a spin! I can't wait.

Finally, Sunday afternoon is here and I'm itching for some spins with my girl. The kind that make your stomach drop and your grin spread wide. I head for the Mount Cotton Driver Training Centre, practically vibrating with anticipation. This is going to be fun, messy, loud, heart-thumping.

I follow the signs to the skid pan and pull into the car park. A small crowd gathers for the driver's briefing. This is motorsport country. I don't know a soul, but I like it already.

The officials run through safety rules, track etiquette, and the game plan for the afternoon. Once we're released, I drive into the holding area, park up, and sign my name on the running order. A pro driver is on hand to ride shotgun for first-timers. Relief floods through me, because honestly, I have no clue what I'm doing yet.

The first car rolls out. Sprinklers erupt, spraying the track in a shimmering mist. Water pools across the surface, turning the asphalt into a slick playground. The driver creeps into the first bend, then—whip!—the car spins in a perfect circle, tires squealing, engine snarling. My pulse jumps. This is going to be *so* good. And hey, maybe I'll even learn a thing or two for the day I lose grip in the rain.

My turn's getting close. The pro instructor steps out of a car… and smacks his head on the closing door. Hard. He's clearly out of commission for a while. The organizer calls out, anyone here still need a teacher? I throw my hand up. He says I might have to wait unless someone volunteers to ride along.

A young gentleman steps forward with a grin. "Happy to help." Yes! I thank him like he's just handed me a winning lotto ticket and run to fetch my girl.

At the start line, he hops in, eyes sweeping over the cockpit. "Nice ride," he says. "Suits you." I flash a grin, fire up the engine, and switch to manual mode. Safety features? Off. Every single one.

It's just us, the wet track, and my heartbeat in my ears. I roll toward the first corner. "Slower," he says. I *thought* I was slow. "Slower," he repeats. Fine. Then—"Now throttle! Turn the wheel!"

It sounds simple. It is not simple. My timing's off. My speed's off. I'm laughing, he's laughing, and my girl's tail is twitching like she's ready to bite.

Coming up to the next corner, I give it another go, foot down, wheel turned, and she *almost* spins. Closer. Better. I can feel it.

Third time lucky. I ease her in, slow and deliberate, then slam the throttle, crank the wheel, YES! She whips around in a perfect spin, tires shrieking, water spraying in an arc across the track. I squeal like a kid on a roller coaster, high-pitched and shameless. My heart is pounding, my cheeks ache from grinning. I've just lost complete control of my car, wrestled it back, and loved every single second.

Fifteen minutes of heaven. Slow crawl, sudden surge, spin, straighten, over and over, until the world becomes a blur of motion and sound.

And then… it's over. Time gone in a flash. I'm already counting down to my next turn.

My track guide grins at me. "Want to ride shotgun in my session?" Yes, please! His weapon of choice? A BMW M3 Competition. I slide into the passenger seat like I'm boarding a fighter jet. This thing's a rolling computer, bristling with driving programs, one built *just* for this madness.

We launch into the first bend and he spins it effortlessly, controlled chaos, pure precision. I'm laughing, hanging on, and realizing this man clearly knows his craft. After all, he just taught me to do it.

While I'm waiting for my next run, a flash of vibrant pink catches my eye. A woman with hair the colour of candyfloss walks straight over and introduces herself. She's the coordinator for the interclub racing challenges. "We need more women in motorsport," she says, watching my wide grin. "Interested in racing for the club?"

"YES," I reply with no hesitation. I'm in. She walks me through the events, the licenses I'll need, the gear, the rules. I'm listening, but my mind is already picturing the grid, the roar of engines, the flag dropping.

I came here for a skid pan session. I'm leaving with the first spark of a racing career.

Over the course of the afternoon, I get a few more chances to fling my girl sideways. Each time I nail a perfect spin, I let out a squeal that could probably be heard from the parking lot. My tutor rides along again, calling tips between laughs, and by the last run, we're working like a team. I've made a good friend here, and had one of the best days of my life.

Honestly? Joining this club might just be the best decision I've made all year.

Back home, I don't even kick off my shoes before flipping open the laptop. The club's event calendar lights up my screen, track days, hill climbs, more skid pan sessions, and I start adding them all to mine.

I register for the licenses I'll need to race my street car, legally, on an actual racetrack.

Some people stumble into hobbies. I think I just drifted into mine, sideways, grinning, and absolutely hooked. Now maybe I will have something to replace the alcohol. It is killing me and I have to win.

Monday, 4 July. **Day one**. This time, I'm serious. I commit, no half-measures, to doing my own detox.

I make it through the day. At 3:00 p.m., the moment I get home from work, I take my first dose of Diazepam. 5:30 p.m, I log into the Recovery Zoom meeting. It's a good one, solid advice, useful resources I can dive into later. I'm looking forward to *not* drinking. I even scout out a few extra meetings to help me survive these fragile first weeks.

I know the key: retrain my brain. Build new habits from 4:30 p.m. onwards. Basically, a routine. I *should* know this already, but knowing and doing are two different beasts.

Day two. The anxiety churns under my skin, but I stay strong. I'm not giving in. I ride the wave, holding my breath until it passes.

Day three. It hits me, *I want a drink.* I've done two whole days, and the voice in my head starts its sweet talk. *What's the harm? You've done well. You deserve it.*

By the time I'm driving home, I've decided: I'll stop at the bottle shop. I'll grab a bottle of wine. I tell myself I'm not going to beat myself up about it, one day at a time, right? I'm bloody impressed I made it two days. No drama, no stress.

That's the story my alcoholic brain feeds me. And, God help me, I buy it.

Day four. My head throbs the moment I open my eyes, yesterday's drinks sour in my stomach. The Diazepam fog wraps around my thoughts, dulling me into someone I don't recognize. I hate it.

I throw the towel in. Two days clean, then I blew it. I decide: next week, no drinking from Sunday to Wednesday. It's not perfect, but it's a fight plan. Failure presses in, but I shove it back. I'll keep swinging. One day, I'll land the final hit.

The weekend is here and it's my second BMW club event, a leisurely drive to a lunch destination being a winery up in the mountains, and I'm buzzing with excitement. Early Saturday morning, we gather at our designated meeting spot, coffee cups in hand, twenty gleaming BMWs lined up like an automotive rainbow, each model a little different but all united by that unmistakable badge. The winter air is crisp enough to bite at my cheeks, the sky a flawless, endless blue. I keep the roof of my convertible closed, it's too chilly for all that fresh air just yet.

Engines purr and rumble to life, a low chorus of power. We roll out, single file, through the cane fields around Jacobs Well, the sweet, earthy scent of sugarcane lingering in the cool air. It's follow-the-leader, but not too close, I want space to let my girl stretch her legs. Sports mode engaged, she growls with each acceleration, hugging the road like she knows she was born for it.

Our route then winds through the sleepy suburbs of Pimpama, Yatala, and Wolfedene, where houses doze quietly behind neat hedges. Then the road tilts upward, twisting and coiling into Tamborine Mountain. Ferns fan out along the roadside, their emerald fronds glistening in the filtered light, and tropical plants stand tall like sentries guarding a rainforest kingdom.

The winery comes into view at last, a postcard-perfect property with rows of grapevines stretching into the distance, their bare winter branches etched against the pale horizon. Lunch is a slow, easy affair, clinking glasses, plates fragrant with fresh bread and rich cheeses, and conversations flowing with my new tribe of like-minded, classic car lovers.

I meet quite a few people from the club, most are leisure drivers, not motorsport inclined, and the conversation has a different flavour today. I'm loving it. I've found two niches I fit into perfectly.

Two hours later, engines roar to life once more, and we snake back down the mountain toward home.

I wake with a rare burst of confidence, certain I won't drink today. The morning feels light, almost airy, until midday arrives and something in me shifts, silently, without warning. By lunchtime, the conviction is gone. I don't know why.

Tomorrow night, I'm going out to dinner, so I draw a line in the sand. Tonight I'll drink, but tomorrow, I won't. I plan for Tuesday and Thursday to be AFDs (alcohol-free days). Or maybe I should just wait until I'm in Tassie and do a full detox there. Five days. That sounds cleaner, more final. But the truth is, I need to start cutting down now, if only to make it easier when the real quitting comes.

The next few days dissolve into a blur, scrolling, reading and obsessing. My phone screen becomes a dim blue window into every horror alcohol can cause: the bloated liver, the frayed neurons, the slow decay of skin and spirit. I've known all this for years. But until now, I didn't care. And that, more than the drinking, terrifies me.

I search for a magic key, something that might snap my mind into place. A new tactic. A sharper truth. But nothing lands. Nothing tells me how to save myself from dying.

My mind is made up, I'll wait until the end of the month when I'm in Tassie. I'll detox there. I'll give up there.

This week, I have something else to focus on, my first motorsport event, Saturday at the Lakeside Park Driver Training Centre (DTC). I pay my entry fee, sign the forms, and tick every box on the paperwork. Now I just need a helmet. My son has a couple, so I arrange to borrow one of his.

It's race day, I pull into Lakeside DTC bright and early, the morning air sharp and smelling faintly of petrol and cut grass. My nerves bubble like the idling engines around me. I find the rest of the team, and my lovely pink-haired friend walks me through prepping the car. The tow hook is screwed firmly in place, a red triangular sticker marking the front. A blue triangle on the bonnet shows the battery location. My race number clings proudly to the window.

Racewear: long pants, enclosed shoes, a long-sleeved cotton shirt, and the all-important helmet. I'm zipped, strapped, and buzzing with anticipation. The course is short but tricky, a tight loop of asphalt, lined with traffic cones like orange sentinels. The goal: follow the set direction, don't hit the cones, they are there to show you where the edge drops off the track. We'll go out one at a time, the clock our only opponent.

The adrenaline is already building. My hands itch to grip the wheel.

I watch a few drivers tear through the course, their tyres screeching, engines snarling. I'm studying every move, every line they take, but my stomach is already flipping with anticipation. It looks challenging. It looks fast. It looks fun.

Then it's my turn.

I roll into position, heart thudding against my ribs. The air smells of hot rubber and high-octane fuel. My hands are slick on the wheel. Oh God, this is it. I have no idea what I'm doing, but somehow, it feels exactly right.

Adrenaline floods my veins as I flick the girl into sports mode. I fix my eyes on the green light, my foot hovering over the accelerator.

The light changes.

I slam the pedal down. The engine roars, and I shoot forward, the G-force pinning me to the seat. Up the first hill, into a tight right-hand turn, tyres grip hard, body leaning, corner one nailed. A squeal escapes me before I can stop it, half laughter, half pure thrill.

Another bend, a short burst of straight, and then, the donut. One massive, glorious circle of smooth cement. I hug the inside line, the wheel tugging in my hands, going as fast as I dare. The back end slips just enough for a cheeky drift, my stomach lurching in delight. I power out of it, hit another short straight, flick through two more corners, and then the straight to finish the course.

I bury the accelerator. The car surges, the world blurring at the edges, engine howling. The finish line rushes up, and I slam the brakes the instant I cross. My pulse is a drumbeat in my ears.

Oh. My. God.

That was insane. I want more. I want to go faster next time.

Every run sharpens me. The lines get cleaner, the turns smoother, the straights faster. My confidence swells with every lap, feeding something wild and hungry inside me. I'm hooked, this is my new addiction, and it's pure, high-octane joy.

By the end of the day, I've racked up ten runs. Each one feels like a personal victory, my times tumbling lower and lower. I can feel the car and I syncing, the way a heartbeat syncs with breath, every shift, every brake, every surge forward sharper than the last.

Speed is no longer just thrilling. It's intoxicating.

The next event is also at Lakeside Park, but this time on the main race track, a regularity challenge organized by the BMW Club to raise money for charity. Entries are already closed, so I can't compete, but they're offering something called *Happy Laps* before the official racing starts. The second I hear about it, I sign up. It means I'll get to take my girl onto the main circuit and drive very, very fast.

The week crawls by. My plans to cut down on drinking? Gone. I drink as much as ever. I really have taken a step back! Then finally, Sunday arrives. *Happy Laps Day.*

I'm at the track before the sun has burned off the morning haze. Engines growl in the background as I check in for the driver's briefing. The rules are simple: no overtaking, no excessive speeding. *Hmm…okay.*

Race gear on, helmet secure, I roll into line with the other cars. My stomach flips in anticipation as the marshal waves us forward.

And then—we're off.

The moment my tyres touch the main track, it's like stepping into a dream. I've watched countless Supercars scream around this very circuit on TV, and now I'm here, my hands on the wheel, my girl purring beneath me. The first turns, I take easy, letting the car and I learn the rhythm, feeling out the lines.

Then, there it is. The corner that leads into the massive straight.

I drop my foot.

The engine roars, the speed climbs 120, 140, 160, the world tightening into a tunnel ahead of me. At 170 kilometres an hour, the air feels alive, pressing against the car like an invisible wall. I ease off just before the end, the next corner rushing up fast.

No speeding, not me! I am now looking forward to the day I can really hit the higher speeds.

Three days to go until I fly to Tassie, and I'm still buzzing from the Lakeside Park drive. My head is spinning, adrenaline coursing through my veins. But now a thought lodges and won't budge: I really have to give up drinking. I can't be racing with alcohol in my system, that's not just risky, it's downright stupid and not to mention illegal.

CHAPTER NINTEEN

The Brink of Self Destruction

Finally, Wednesday arrives. I board the plane bound for Tasmania, celebrating Mum's birthday this time, she will be turning eighty on the thirtieth. We'll spend a couple of days at Cradle Mountain to mark the occasion. I make a silent pact: detox begins on July 30, a day worthy of a clean start.

The moment I walk into Mum's place, I'm popping the cork off a bottle. Then another. I tell myself I'm making the most of my "last days."

Friday comes, and we head for Cradle Mountain. I have packed two bottles of wine, my *very last* drinks, I swear. The drive takes us two hours from Launceston, first along the open highway toward Deloraine then soon we're climbing into the snow-capped mountains, winding past walls of lush green ferns and towering trees. Tiny storybook towns, Mole Creek, Mount Roland and Moina slip by in the rearview mirror. We pass King Solomon's Caves, their entrances hidden behind curtains of moss, beckoning explorers.

The curves straighten, and we break out onto the plains of Cradle Mountain–Lake St Clair National Park. The landscape suddenly feels alien, flat and sparse, like a scene from Mars. Small shrubs huddle low to the earth; the colours are earthy browns, muted greens, and soft beige. This is known as wombat country, we scan the roadside, hoping to spot one grazing.

The turnoff to Cradle Mountain comes, and the scenery transforms again. Green shrubs cluster thickly, King Billy and ancient Huon pines guarding the road. Snow drifts rest quietly in the gullies, tucked into shadows.

A short climb later, we arrive at the village we will be staying at. A few more turns and our cabin comes into view, a little hideaway nestled among the native trees. Outside, small mounds of snow; inside, blissful warmth, thank God, I hate the cold. We get a bedroom each, there is a large lounge, a compact kitchen, and a shared bathroom. Double glass doors open onto a covered balcony where ghost gums stretch skyward. Birds land on the railing, feathers ruffling in the breeze, and pademelons hop past like we've stepped into a nature documentary.

We drop our bags on our beds and head straight back out to explore. Just a short drive away is the Cradle Mountain Tavern, where a crackling open fire waits, flanked by deep lounge chairs perfect for sinking into with a glass of mulled wine and a hearty meal.

We park and set off on the Enchanted Forest Walk, a 1.1-kilometre circuit that winds through a fairytale world. Moss carpets the ground and clings to the trunks of ancient trees. Tiny bursts of orange, red, and yellow fungi punctuate the green. Wooden bridges arch over a cascading creek, the water rushing and chattering as it tumbles downstream. Along the path, we spot the famously odd square-shaped wombat droppings, and not long after, we see the culprit, a plump wombat nibbling on moss just a metre from the trail, completely unfazed by our presence.

Then, as if the mountain is showing off, snow begins to fall. Soft flakes drift down, melting on my cheeks. For Mum, it's a dream fulfilled. She's been chasing snow on Cradle Mountain for years but has never been caught in it as it falls. Now she's squealing with delight, spinning in circles like a kid on a carnival ride. Her cheeks glow pink, her eyes sparkle, and for a moment I just watch her, feeling the magic of it seep into me too.

After the walk, the tavern calls us in with its warmth. We thaw out by the fire, mulled wine for Mum, champagne for me, I'm still making the most of my "last days" of drinking.

The next morning, Mum's birthday arrives. My brother and sister-in-law have arranged to drive up for lunch as a surprise. I book a table at the tavern for 11:30 so they can sneak in first, hang balloons, and hand the cake over to the kitchen. Mum and I stroll in at midday, none the wiser, until *Surprise!* They leap out from behind the fireplace, and Mum's face lights up brighter than the candles will later.

Today is the day I swore I'd stop drinking. But my alcoholic brain argues otherwise: *It's a celebration. Just start tomorrow.* I listen, of course.

Lunch is a feast. Woodfired pizzas arrive, their blistered crusts carrying the irresistible scent of smoke and char. Grilled halloumi squeaks under my teeth, salty and rich. Coleslaw crunches, dressed sharp and tangy. Spicy chicken wings land with a fiery aroma that makes my eyes water before I even take a bite. And then, the cake. Sweet, dense, perfect. Champagne bubbles in my glass, wine flows, craft beer froths in pints. The fire roars just metres away, wrapping us all in its glow as laughter bounces off the timber walls.

After lunch, the others head back down the mountain, leaving Mum and me with one last night in our cabin. And here's my problem: I only packed two bottles of wine, and I polished them off last night. I need two more to get me through tonight.

At the tavern bar, I ask if they sell bottles to take away. They do, but at twice the price of a bottle shop. I wince, but I hand over the money. The need outweighs the sting in my purse.

Back at the cabin, the evening is quiet. Mum settles in front of the TV, wrapped in a blanket, her eyes on some British crime show. I curl up in the lounge, the heater cranked up high, glass in hand. I drink until the familiar buzz settles in and the rest of the world recedes. Tomorrow, I tell myself, is a new day.

The trip ends, and we head back down the mountain in no hurry, winding past the ferns and snow drifts, the little towns and the open plains. By the time we reach Mum's, my resolve to stop drinking here has vanished, I'll start when I get home, I tell myself.

That afternoon, I fly back to Brisbane, drop my bags upstairs in my room, pour myself a drink and I sit there, glass in hand, wondering what the hell I'm going to do to stop.

A plan comes to me, something I read in one of the many recovery books I've devoured: journal a "typical drinking session." Fine. Let's do this, Jane.

At 4:30 p.m. I start drinking, I start writing: **First drink**—Relief. Warmth blooms in my chest. My shoulders loosen, the noise in my head fades.

Twenty minutes later: **Second drink**—More relaxed now, thoughts floating free. I start thinking maybe I'm not so broken after all.

Fifteen minutes later: **Third drink**—My vision wobbles slightly. I notice and don't care.

By 8:00 p.m.—Two bottles gone. I'm drunk, I shower, crawl into bed, and pass out.

The next morning, I wake disoriented. I don't remember cooking dinner. Or eating it. Or having a shower. Or getting into bed. Seeing the words I wrote the night before makes it real. And that terrifies me.

That night after work, I try the book's next suggestion: journal how I feel after drinking. I write about the mental fog, the guilt, the bloating, the pimples blooming along my jaw, the shame, the self-hate that seeps into everything.

Then I document the next drinking session. Same times. Same quantities. Same ending.

For two more weeks, I keep going, every night the same blurred pattern. I barely remember writing the entries I read the next day. I'm running on autopilot, my body in full revolt, my mind somewhere far behind.

It's mid-August, and I decide, again, to try and self-detox. The next day, I back out. Terror grips me. What if I get the shakes? Heart palpitations? Have a seizure? The truth hits hard once again: I can't do this alone.

I start searching for detox facilities that offer short-term stays, three to seven days. That's all I need, right? Just a little help to push through the worst of it. Then I'll be done. I'll never drink again.

What a joke.

I start calling around. Every place says the same thing: minimum admission is fourteen days. One facility offers twenty-eight days, my health insurance won't cover it but it's fully funded by the Department of Veteran Affairs (DVA) because I'm a veteran, I am eligible for this. But there's a catch with this facility: attendance at Alcoholics Anonymous (AA) meetings is mandatory.

Oh, hell no.

I hang up.

By the end of August, I've smashed into another rock bottom. Work is slipping through my fingers, my performance in freefall. I'm spiraling, watching myself crumble in real time. This isn't just drinking anymore, this is destruction. I am about to lose everything.

I call the rehab back. The same one I'd hung up on.

A calm, steady voice answers. I tell her I called the other day wanting to know about the program and about my resistance to AA, bracing for judgment. But she listens, she explains gently that AA doesn't have to be religious unless I want it to be, that it's simply a support system, a place to not be alone.

I'm desperate. And I know if I don't get help now, I won't be here much longer.

So I say yes.

But it's not instant. They can't take me for ten days. The thought of waiting feels unbearable, like standing on a cliff edge with the ground crumbling under my feet. But there's nothing I can do except agree.

The next day, a miracle.

They call me, there's a spot opening in four days.

"Yes," I blurt, almost shouting into the phone.

Relief floods me, I make the arrangements. Once again, I walk into my manager's office and tell him I need four weeks off to go back to rehab. He doesn't hesitate, he knows I am at rock bottom and approves my leave request on the spot, assures me he understands, and that we'll sort things out. God bless him.

Then I call my family. Their relief is immediate, almost audible over the line. I hadn't realised the extent of their worry over my attempts to self-detox, and shame burns through me. I hate that I've put them through this.

But that shame steals my resolve. This time, I will get it right. I have to.

PART FOUR
The Fourth Rehab

CHAPTER TWENTY

The Turning Point

August 31, 2022. Bags packed again. This time, there's no little red Getz to whisk me off to yet another shot at sobriety. Instead, I'm heading two and a half hours north of Brisbane and the Department of Veteran Affairs (DVA) has arranged my transport as part of my treatment deal.

My ride arrives, this is it, my last hope. If I don't get it right this time, I don't think there's anything left in me to try again. I need this to work.

The journey north is long and quiet. I watch the highway unravel beneath me, the scenery shifting from urban sprawl to lush countryside. When the car finally pulls in, I see it: the facility where I'll spend the next twenty eight days. It sits nestled among eucalyptus trees and gentle hills, not far from the coast. The air smells cleaner here, earthy and sharp with gum leaves. But the first thing that catches my eye is the emergency bay and its stark sign: Ambulances stop here.

Serious stuff.

The front half of the facility is the hospital. This is where I'll stay, because I need to detox under medical supervision again. I open the boot, grab my bags, and take a deep breath before heading up the steps to reception. The woman at the desk looks up, I give my name, she smiles politely and asks me to wait and tells me "someone will be out shortly".

A nurse appears soon after and beckons me to follow her. We walk into the hospital, a single-level building with a wide corridor lined with patient rooms. Halfway down is the nurses" station, a functional setup with a counter in front and a medication room tucked off to the side. Behind that are three offices. She leads me into one of them, and we sit to begin the admission paperwork.

Same questions, same answers, I'm practically fluent in this language now. But this time, I'm scared, truly scared. I can't do this anymore. I tear up, as usual, but something's different. The nurse sees it. She leans in, her tone softer, steadier. She gets it, because she's been there. They all have. Everyone who works here are ex addicts, they are in recovery, and that changes everything. I know I'm in the right place.

We go over the rules, the policies, the expectations. She takes my medications, they'll be dispensed as needed. Then she searches my bags for alcohol, drugs and any other contraband. Last, she asks for my mobile phone, it's going into a locked safe for the duration of my stay. No incoming calls allowed, my family and friends can call and enquire after me, but I cannot call them until my allotted time and that is ten days away!!!

She shows me to my room, located in the hospital's left wing. I step inside and take it in: a single bed, a small table, a set of drawers, a cupboard with shelving and a frosted window. The en suite bathroom holds a large shower with no door or curtain, a toilet, and a sink. I notice the taps, they're shaped like diamonds on their sides, awkward to turn. I ask about them. She tells me they're designed that way on purpose, to prevent anything being tied around them.

Now I look closer, there's nowhere in this room where you could fasten anything. Nothing to anchor a rope, a belt, or a sheet. Suicide-proof.

It's stark. It's safe. It's real.

And I'm here.

I leave my bags behind for now, unpacking can wait, and follow the nurse into the main part of the complex. We step into a massive dining hall, easily the largest I've seen in any rehab. It reminds me of a school camp, complete with long tables and a high, echoey wooden raked ceiling.

I glance around and ask, "How many people are here right now?"

"Sixty-five," she replies.

Sixty-five? My jaw nearly drops. Where do they fit them all? She explains that at the back of the buildings there's additional accommodation, dormitory-style. One dorm for the women, one for the men. Yep. Just like camp.

She gives me the grand tour, the dining hall flows into the kitchen area. There's a chef, but she only cooks dinner from Sunday to Friday. Lunch is DIY, salads, sandwich makings, fruit, whatever you can throw together. It's lunchtime now, so she tells me to help myself. I grab some ingredients and make a toasted sandwich, the familiar crunch and sizzle oddly comforting.

As I eat, people start straggling in from classes. They introduce themselves one by one, some warm, others skeptical. I hear both the good and the bad. It's strict here, there are rules, lots of them. It feels more like prison than rehab.

"We all have chores," someone tells me. "There's a roster. You serve meals, clean, sweep, whatever's listed. Make sure to check it every day."

My first impression? What the actual fuck have I signed up for? This isn't like any program I've done before. But maybe that's a good thing, maybe different is what I need.

After lunch, I head back to the nurses" station for the mandatory doctor's appointment. He'll prescribe the Diazepam I need for detox and check over my general health. I wait a bit, then go into his office and, once again, rattle off the greatest hits of my history: alcohol, depression, anxiety, the works.

We finish up and I move to another office where a nurse draws blood for the standard tests. Routine stuff, let's see if I have done any more damage to my poor liver.

Back at the nurses' station, it's time for medication (meds) and observations (obs). Thank God, two pills 10 milligrams (mg) each of Diazepam four times today, a total of 80mg wow, that's more than previous detox's. I cradle the little white cup like it holds salvation, this will help ease the anxiety gnawing through my chest.

I sit still while she wraps the plastic cuff of the blood pressure monitor around my arm. I close my eyes. I know it's high, dangerously high.

She confirms it with a quiet gasp. "Well, that is high."

No kidding.

"Don't worry," she says. "It'll come down. Just relax and go with the program. Don't fight it."

I nod, trying to believe her.

But truthfully? I have no idea what I'm in for yet.

Finally medicated, I return to my room, ready for that relaxing feeling, ready to unpack and take all of this in. "Here I go again," is the only thing running through my head. Slowly, I begin to put my things away, arranging them just enough to make the room feel a little more like mine. A flicker of familiarity, something to lift my spirits.

The nurse checks in again and, seeing I've unpacked, offers to show me the communal lounge room we get to watch TV. That's a win.

I sink into the lounge and flick through the channels, searching for something light and mind-numbing. Something that will let my brain go quiet for a while. She says I'll get a full tour of the rest of the facility later.

A couple of ladies come into the room and introduce themselves. They only arrived yesterday, still finding their footing too. As we chat, I learn one's ex-Navy, the other ex-Army. I smile. "I'm ex-Air Force."

We all laugh. That instant camaraderie only service people understand snaps into place.

Now comes the part where I have to accept a hard fact: this rehab is heavily based on Alcoholics Anonymous (AA) and Narcotics Anonymous (NA). We're expected to attend a meeting every single day.

It's Wednesday, and tonight's meeting will be held here in one of the classrooms. It's a Zoom session, others who have left here and now at the halfway house and previous residents out on their own, will be dialing in. But I won't be attending, not yet, I'm on Diazepam, and that's considered a mind-altering substance. No meetings for me until detox is nearly complete.

The lounge begins to fill with more people from the hospital wing. One by one, I'm introduced. There's one thing we all share: we're addicts. Different stories. Different poisons. Same bloody fight. Same shitty disease.

It's strange how comforting that is.

Here, I'm not the odd one out. I don't have to explain or pretend or soften the truth. No one's shocked when I say I've relapsed four spectacular times. No one flinches at the word *detox*.

We all know what rock bottom looks like, we've each been there, or close enough to smell it.

And now we're here, trying to claw our way back up.

It's 5:30 p.m., dinner time. I trail behind a few of the girls into the dining room. They're showing me the ropes, walking me through the evening routine like seasoned pros. We settle around the long tables, already set with cutlery, plastic cups, salt and pepper shakers, jugs of cordial that smells faintly of childhood and artificial strawberries. The dinner roster crew has done the setup; they'll also be on cleanup duty afterward.

I sit with my new friends, trying to act like this is normal. One of the support workers steps forward and starts roll call. Roll call! I can't help but laugh to myself, this really does feel like school camp.

Once we've all been marked present, we go around the table, each person sharing two things they're grateful for. It's easier than I expect, I'm genuinely grateful for the chance to piece my life back together and for the people already making me feel less alone.

We line up at the counter in front of the kitchen, a row of steaming bain-maries waits behind it. The kitchen duty crew stand ready, scooping food onto our plates with that practiced rhythm I'm starting to recognize. For a moment, it feels more like jail than school camp. I take my tray and sit down. The meal? Not bad, very homely. That's a win in my book.

When we're done, we scrape the leftovers into a bin and hand our plates through the window into the washing-up area. The "inmates", yes, that's what I'm calling us, rinse and load everything into the industrial dishwasher.

With dinner done, it's free time until the on-site meeting starts at 7:00 p.m. I head back to the hospital wing with the others. We're not allowed in the rest of the facility unless we're living in the dorms or attending a scheduled class.

When it's time for the meeting, those cleared to attend head up the hill to the designated room. The rest of us, those still on detox, stay behind. I head off for a hot shower, letting the water wash away the day's tension. It's quiet. Private. I tell the girls I'll catch up with them in the TV lounge afterward.

Clean and in fresh clothes, I check in at the nurses' station for obs and my evening meds. Then I curl into one of the lounge chairs, as I wait for other detoxees to arrive and keep me company.

Just after 8:00 p.m., the others return from the Zoom meeting. We hang out for a bit, chatting, laughing, getting to know each other in that easy, slow way strangers do when they're all starting over.

Lights-out is 11:00 p.m., but I tap out early at 10:00 p.m. I've got 80 milligrams of Diazepam coursing through my system, and I'm melting into calm. My first day is over. I feel… safe.

CHAPTER TWENTY ONE

The Rules

The morning arrives bright and biting. We're tucked into the mountains, so the day begins wrapped in mist, with crisp air that stings my nose and smells like eucalyptus and damp earth. I've been told bootcamp starts every morning at 7.30 a.m. sharp. I dig out my gym gear that hasn't seen the light of day since my last half-hearted training stint, and head to the dining area, which doubles as our muster point.

Roll call again. These people do not miss a beat. Once we're accounted for, we're told to walk or run up the road to the front gate, a distance of one kilometre - round trip. Twice. Relief floods me. Walking, I can do. I fall into a steady pace, chatting with a few others as we move. The road cuts through the countryside, tree-lined, peaceful, beautiful. The air is so clean it almost tastes sweet.

Bootcamp done, we've got until 9:00 a.m. to shower, eat breakfast, and get ready for the day. I'm heading to my first classroom session next. No idea what to expect, but I'm curious. And a little excited, this could be the start of something.

All refreshed, I head to the nurses' station for my morning meds and obs. Everything's pretty much the same as yesterday, which is a relief. My Diazepam dose has been halved today down to 40mg: 10mg at a time instead of 20mg. I'm handed the familiar little white cup holding one tiny tablet. Alongside it, the nurse gives me two sachets of instant coffee.

"This has to last you all day," she says, half-apologetic.

What the hell!! We are on coffee rations. I am in jail! Oh well at least we get some unlike the last place, I will have to make them last.

Medicated and holding my precious sachets, I make my way to the dining room for breakfast. It's a help-yourself setup again: cereal, toast, fruit. I go with cereal, find a tub of yogurt in the communal fridge, and top it off with a bit of chopped fruit. I nurse my coffee like it's gold dust.

By 9:00 a.m., it's time to face the classroom. I have no idea what's coming, but I'm ready for anything right now.

As we file in, we're immediately divided into two groups. One of the support workers explains that it's time for check-in, and there are too many of us for one person to handle, hence the split. The classroom is stark white, with laminated slogans about recovery on the walls, the desks are set into a U shape so when we sit down we are all looking at each other. I've done group check-ins before, but this one's got its own spin. A stack of laminated sheets are passed around, each covered in emojis and mood descriptions. We're told to use them to help name two emotions on what we're feeling today.

When it's my turn, I don't hesitate. "Anxious and excited," I say.

That's it. Done. And honestly? That feels good.

As I listen to the others go around, I start picking up on the energy in the room. Some strong personalities, some fragile ones, and a whole lot of emotion swirling beneath the surface. It's a little intimidating. Okay, it's a lot intimidating.

After check-in, we're ushered to the main building for a farewell ceremony. Anyone finishing their time at the facility gets a heartfelt send-off. Support workers give speeches, family members can attend, and there's cake. Actual cake. YES. The ceremonies are held in the seniors' class room at the top of the clinic, a very comfortable room, the walls and ceiling are lined with warm timber, large tables are placed in front of the windows, catching as much light as possible.

Apparently, this happens most days. People are always coming and going, so farewells become part of the rhythm here.

By the time we return to the classroom, it's 10:30 a.m., and now comes the serious part, the expectations talk.

The facilitator of the class in the detox unit (us in the hospital) is a rugged looking man who is of course in recovery, as all the staff here are. He introduces himself and says he will be running all of the classes here in the unit. I like immediately, he is down to earth, honest and relatable and he has been clean and sober for ten years!

He lays the rules out, one by one. No exceptions, one wrong move, and you're out.

Respect is non-negotiable. Chores are mandatory when rostered. No relationships allowed, absolutely no co-mingling in the dorms. If you're caught in someone else's room, especially with someone of the opposite sex, you'll be asked to leave. No second chances.

Wow.

The message is clear: this place runs on structure, accountability, and boundaries, I'm okay with that.

The morning has disappeared, it's lunchtime already. Off we go to the dining room and today I see there are a couple of quiches on the main table, the chef must have whipped them up last night for our lunch. I hone in on that, grab a slice before it is all gone, then proceed to make a toasted sandwich.

I talk to a few people I haven't met yet, they are from the "seniors section", yep long-timers, those who've stayed past the initial four weeks to complete the full three-month program. They're... something else. They know all of the gossip, what you can get away with and what you can't. It's like being thrown back into year Seven camp, only everyone's a grown-up with trauma and other issues.

Note to self: Keep your cool, Jane. Don't get involved in the drama.

Lunch is done, an experience all on its own, and I'm back in the classroom, stomach full, brain foggy, and already wondering what other lessons we are in for.

This session is a "steps" lesson. Yep. Here we go, the AA part of the program. The topic today? Step One.

We admitted we were powerless over alcohol—that our lives had become unmanageable.

Well, shit. That's me. Word for word!

I sit a little straighter in my chair. My skin prickles, not from discomfort, but from recognition. I've done this step before, eight years ago, I just didn't realize it had a name. Didn't know it was part of something bigger. Now, I feel strangely at ease. Maybe I can listen to this AA "nonsense" after all.

Maybe I'm more ready than I thought.

I listen eagerly as Mr Rugged reads through the rest of the information on this first step and I am actually looking forward to exploring this more. As the day comes to a close, I am feeling hopeful, this experience is certainly full of surprises.

Thursday night's AA and NA meetings are held in Maroochydore, a coastal town about an hour and a half away. The rehab operates four light commercial buses to transport everyone to the meetings. Four senior residents are rostered to drive, and we're each assigned to a specific bus before departure. Since I'm still in detox, I'm not permitted to attend these meetings yet, but I'm told I'll get to experience them next week. Four out of the seven weekly meetings take place off-site.

Day three (Friday) begins with boot camp, two brisk walks to the front gate and back, lungs filling with crisp morning air, shoes crunching against gravel. Then it's off to the nurses' station for meds and obs. I'm being cut down to 20mg of Diazepam today, so I get my little white cup with one pale tablet inside; the other one will come later this afternoon.

Coffee rations in hand, I head into breakfast. It's the same as yesterday, but with a bonus, muesli bars! I grab one and tuck it away for later, feeling like I've scored something special.

At 9:00 a.m., it's time for morning check-in, and I'm still going strong. Today, I receive my AA literature, a fresh copy of *Alcoholics Anonymous* (the Big Book) and the Twelve Steps, split into three workbooks I can write in. Some of the others here are fighting drugs instead of alcohol, so they're given the NA version.

As Mr Rugged explains the concept, something clicks. This isn't what I thought it would be. The higher power they talk about, it's not necessarily God. It can be anything greater than myself. I can definitely work with that. The way it's explained actually makes sense: a higher power is anything stronger than you. I decide, right then and there, that mine is the ocean. It's vast, it moves things, it sustains life, and it calms me. Yes, easy.

By 10:00 a.m., it's time to say goodbye to a few more people, which means… cake. I've saved my second sachet of coffee for this moment, sipping it slowly while we celebrate (eat cake) and send them off. The goodbyes stretch on, so we head straight to lunch afterward.

This afternoon is Art Therapy, my absolute favourite. It's held in the same big, airy room where we do farewells. It has been transformed into an art wonderland, paints, feltpens, paper, boxes, beads, old jewelry and fabrics scattered on all of the tables. I decide to make a necklace today, threading alphabet and colourful beads into something meaningful. I spell out the names of my son, my daughter-in-law, and my grandchildren, each name a reminder of why I'm going to succeed this time. I wear them close to my heart.

Later, we gather for meditation in the recreation room, my first time here. It's downstairs from the dining hall, with timber-paneled walls, a vaulted ceiling, soft carpet underfoot, and huge windows overlooking a wide green oval bordered by gum trees. Beyond that, the highway rumbles with the distant promise of Brisbane.

We sprawl out across the floor, some on yoga mats, others on blankets. A few even bring pillows. The instructor's voice is soft and steady, guiding us into an hour-long meditation. I don't last. I fall asleep. And honestly? It's perfect.

Dinner follows the same ritual as the night before, roll call, gratitude, and eat. The dining hall is busy with the low buzz of conversation, forks clinking against plates, chairs scraping back as people finish their meals and drift into their evening routines.

Tonight, though, I've been granted permission to attend the on-site meeting at 7:00 p.m., what they call a Hospitals & Institutions meeting, or H & I. Two members from AA or NA are coming in to share their stories. Their journey to sobriety. Where they were. Where they are now.

At 6:55 p.m., I arrive at the meeting room. A couple of senior residents stand by the door like sentinels, and, hallelujah, they're handing out coffee sachets. Yes please. I don't usually drink coffee at night, but nothing about this is usual. This is rehab, this is war, and coffee is my armor. I tear open a sachet and dump it into my cup, already halfway to the hot water urn.

I find a seat and settle in, ready to observe. This meeting, I'm told, happens every Friday night.

The two guest speakers sit at the front of the room. One by one, they share their stories, raw, unfiltered, full of ache and triumph. It's heartbreaking. And somehow, it's also exactly what I need. A reminder that this isn't impossible. That people do recover. That maybe I can, too.

At the end, a support worker stands up to thank them. We clap, grateful, stirred. Then he turns to us and says, "Take on board what you've heard tonight. Out of everyone in this room, only one percent of you will succeed and not relapse."

What. The. Fuck.

I'm horrified. Did he seriously just say that?

Then, almost before I can stop myself, I think, *Well, I'm going to be in that one percent, asshole.*

(Turns out he was right. And so was I).

I head back to my area, check in with the nurses' for final obs and meds, then slip into bed early. My mind is buzzing. So much to think about and so much to feel.

CHAPTER TWENTY TWO

My Breaking Point

Saturday morning comes with no alarm. No boot camp. No classes. But breakfast still needs to be eaten before 9:00 a.m. so the rostered crew can clean up.

I sleep in a little, then shuffle down to the nurses' station for morning obs and meds. I'm down to 10mg of Diazepam today. One tiny 5mg tablet rests in the white plastic cup. The last dose will come later.

The rest of the morning is ours.

I choose to dive into some "homework." I go to the common area which is located next to the dining room, a small space with some comfortable chairs and coffee tables. We've been asked to begin our step work, Steps One through Three. I spread out my workbooks on the table and settle into it, the air still and quiet, save for the occasional rustle of paper or the soft murmur of someone walking by.

I also crack open the AA Book, It was written in 1939 by a man called Bill Wilson. Let's see what this character has to say on how he wrestled his way through this ugly disease and somehow found a way out.

I'm not sure what I'm looking for yet, but I know I'm going to find something.

It's raining today, the kind that drums steadily on the roof and keeps the world gray and soft. No outside activities, so after lunch one of the support workers gathers us in the main recreation room for a group game.

She holds up a giant ball of string and grins. "Everyone on the floor," she says. "We're playing string ball."

We all find a spot on the carpet to sit down. She explains the rules, one person starts by holding the ball of string, throws it to someone else, still holding their end of the string, and as it unravels, the web begins to grow. That person throws to another, then another, until we've built a big, tangled net connecting us all.

Laughter bounces off the walls. People toss the string back and forth, calling names, catching it midair, joking like old friends at a barbecue. It's light. Easy. Until suddenly, it's over.

"Game done!" the worker calls out.

And I sit there, the only person with their hands empty. The ball never came to me.

I laugh with the others, but inside, something caves. I sit still, chin high, fighting the heat behind my eyes. *Why does this always happen to me? Why am I always the one left out?* I'm spiraling, trapped in my own head, and that is *not* a safe neighborhood.

I gather myself, still smiling like I'm fine, and make my way quietly back to my room.

On the way, I remember I left my sunglasses downstairs on a shelf. I head back, hoping no one will notice me. But the support worker is there.

"You okay?" she asks.

And that's all it takes.

I break. The tears come, I let out a sob, fighting to hold it together. She doesn't panic. She just stays with me, talks to me gently, reminds me I'm not alone. I let it all out.

Eventually, I make it back to my room, face blotchy, eyes swollen, a complete mess. But something shifts.

As I lie there, I realize how thankful I am for that retreat I went to last year, for my mental health. Without it, I wouldn't know how to pick myself up again. But I do. I remember how to love myself, I breathe and I reset.

All I need to focus on now is the alcohol. This AA thing? It's going to work. I know it.

Later, a quiet knock comes at my door. A couple of the others, people who must've noticed I was upset, stand there, asking if I'm all right. I try to wave them off, tell them I'm okay, even though I look like hell. But they won't take no for an answer.

"Come for a walk," one of them says.

We walk to the gate and back. We talk. We laugh. The fresh air, the steady rhythm of our steps, the simple kindness, it pulls me back. This camaraderie is something else entirely. We are all on the same page here.

By late afternoon, it's time for the group to head into town for an AA meeting. Everyone goes, except those of us still in detox. It's my last day, so I sit this one out.

I hang in the TV lounge with a few others, the rain still tapping gently on the windows. The place feels quiet, still, like we're in the eye of the storm.

Around 6:00 p.m., I hear it. A ruckus in the hallway. Laughter. Shouting.

"Catch and kill!" someone yells.

Wait—*what?* I follow the noise out of the hospital wing, through the dining room into the kitchen, where everything is set up like a DIY Pizza buffet. Pre made bases, trays of toppings, cheese, sauce, fresh herbs, the works.

So this is catch and kill.

I laugh out loud. What a name for something so simple. I *love* it. And I love pizza.

We line up and build our masterpieces. I layer mine with olives, mushrooms, extra cheese, okay, a *lot* of cheese. The commercial oven is already fired up and waiting, glowing hot. We load in our creations and wait, stomachs growling, eyes tracking the bubbling crusts like hawks.

Catch and kill turns out to be my favourite meal so far.

After dinner, the hospital crew shuffles back to the TV lounge, full bellies and happy, we pick out a movie to watch together. It's the perfect way to end an emotional, messy, beautiful day.

Sunday arrives. Day of rest, they say.

Not likely.

It's *chore* day.

At 10:00 a.m., we're summoned to the dining room where a printed roster is taped to the wall like some cruel twist of fate. A list of names and tasks, who's scrubbing what, who's sweeping where. Slave labor, I think. What the hell is this? No one mentioned I'd have to *clean* the damn place.

But then I roll my eyes at myself. *Oh, Jane, just go with it.*

My name's next to "ablutions, main building."

Fantastic.

We all get stuck in, working like a team of reluctant ants. The support workers keep a sharp eye on us. If it's not done properly, they say, we'll do it again. I don't remember it being this bad at school camp, apparently, this happens every Wednesday, too.

I guess it's about teaching us to take responsibility for our own environment, fine. But still.

The rest of the day is quiet. Not much going on. I'm still not allowed phone calls. When I *am* finally allowed, I'll get one whole fifteen-minute slot to call my family or friends. That's it. No visitors yet either.

With nothing else pulling at me, I head down to the pool area for the first time. It's tucked near the oval, nestled against the bushland. The pool itself is small and clean, surrounded by pale paving stones, shade sails flapping gently in the breeze, a few sun loungers scattered around like lazy punctuation marks. It's peaceful.

Today is Father's Day.

Visitors are allowed for those who've been here long enough. The grounds come alive with picnic blankets, plastic containers filled with homemade food, and kids running barefoot through the grass. Families laugh and share fizzy soft drinks, folding chairs tipped back under the trees. It's beautiful to watch, bittersweet, too.

I sit alone, just observing.

It stings, sure. But it also warms me. Seeing children light up around their dads—it reminds me of what matters.

Eventually, dinner rolls around. It's Sunday Roast night.

Roll call. Gratitude. Line up. Eat. Clean up.

There's a rhythm to it now, like a slow drumbeat. I'm getting used to it.

At 7:00 p.m., I head to the on-site meeting room for the NA gathering. I show up early enough to snag my bonus coffee sachets, yes, they're still a thing, and yes, they're still the highlight of my evenings.

This is my first NA meeting.

It's just us, everyone on-site. The room fills quickly, chairs scraping the floor, cups of instant coffee cradled like lifelines.

Two people sit at the front and open the meeting. It's formal. Structured. Cards are read at designated points. People are invited to share their stories, with a time limit of five to seven minutes so everyone gets a chance.

Then someone calls my name.

Oh no.

My stomach drops. What do I say? I've never done this before.

But I stand up. I speak.

First, I must introduce myself: my name is Jane and I am an alcoholic. Wow, to say that out allowed gives me all sorts of mixed feelings, ashamed is the first one, relieved is the second. I then tell the group briefly of my relentless relationship with alcohol, how I've tried three other rehabs, and how I ended up here. My voice doesn't shake as much as I thought it would, then I thank them for letting me share. There's applause and recognition around the room. It wasn't so bad after all.

I listen closely as others share. Some of their stories are staggering, raw, real and painful. Some of these people are lucky to be here. Lucky to be alive.

I leave the room feeling cracked open and somehow steadier.

This isn't just a program. This is something real.

CHAPTER TWENTY THREE

The All Important Epiphany

Monday dawns, and somehow, it's only my sixth day here. It feels much longer, like I've lived a dozen lifetimes since I walked through that front gate.

I go through the morning ritual: wake, obs, meds, breakfast and check-in. Only this time, there's no white cup waiting for me. No tablets. I'm officially drug-free, no more Diazepam. It feels like a small victory and a heavy responsibility all at once. I'm cleared now to attend all meetings, no more restrictions.

Today also marks my first counselling session. We're meant to have one per week, and mine is scheduled for 10:00 a.m. I report to the reception area in the main building, which is far more inviting than the hospital corridor I know. The timber walls and raked ceilings give it a cozy, almost lodge-like atmosphere, less sterile, more human.

A woman calls my name. I follow her into a small office where she welcomes me with a soft voice and open body language. I settle into the chair across from her, palms damp, heart tight.

And then I begin.

I tell her my story. Here we go again....

My history with alcohol. My past attempts at rehab. I tell her about Saturday's string game, how no one threw the ball to me, how invisible I felt, how quickly I spiraled into that dark, dangerous place inside myself. I say the words I hate admitting aloud: *I felt totally left out. I broke down. I cried. I feel unstable and sad and…*

She nods gently, then asks the question I've been dreading: "Are you having suicidal thoughts?"

Maybe, I say. "I'm just so fucked up."

That's it. That's all it takes. For my own safety, she places me on a "Safety Plan."

It means I'll be watched more closely. I'll have to report to the nurse's station during every break so they can assess my state of mind, check in on my mood. It feels clinical, but I understand. I'm not okay right now. Not really.

And then, another epiphany.

I've been skating around the fire in my last three rehabs, now I am in the fire. I am the phoenix, I will rise from the ashes. I will not die.

The rest of the day passes in a blur. I stumble through it, mind foggy, emotions raw, but I make it. I survive.

After dinner, we head into the town of Gympie for an NA meeting. It's only a ten-minute drive from the center, a quick trip.

The meeting is held in an old church hall, and must be at least eighty years old. It has the kind of charm that only old wooden buildings possess. The main hall is out front, complete with a stage and creaky floorboards. There's a large kitchen at the back and an outhouse tacked on like an afterthought.

As we file inside, we're handed our two bonus sachets of coffee. My evening instantly improves. I make a beeline for the kitchen, pour hot water into my cup, and strike up a conversation with a couple of local women. They've brought biscuits too, real ones. Crumbly and sweet. It's a small gesture that feels like a big kindness.

A quick trip to the outhouse, and it's time to settle in.

I take a seat in the main hall. The chairs are placed in a circle. The lighting is dim. There's a worn-in comfort to it all complete with a musty odour of years gone by. People begin to share. I listen, really listen. Some of these people have clawed their way out of the darkest corners of life, and here they are, still standing.

Still fighting.

I'm in awe.

The meeting wraps up after an hour, and we load back onto the buses, heading toward what's slowly becoming my home away from home.

Before bed, I stop by the nurses' station, just as my safety plan requires. I check in, answer their questions honestly. I'm exhausted, but grateful.

I'm still here.

Still trying.

Tuesday morning hits hard.

I wake up heavy. Sad. The weight of everything settles on me like wet concrete. It's one of *those* mornings, where the ceiling feels too close, and my thoughts chaotic, self-pitying spirals.

What has my life come to?

Yep. I am having a full-blown pity party. Table for one.

But I know this spiral, I've lived it before, and I know it leads nowhere good. I sit on the edge of my bed, take a deep breath, and have a quiet word with myself.

You are here to get better, I remind myself. *So snap out of it, Jane. Give yourself a kick up the bum. Twenty-one days to go. That's the goal. Head down, do the work, get through this.*

So I push forward.

Boot camp, breakfast, check-in, classes, lunch, more classes and dinner. I move through the day like clockwork, determination setting in.

By evening, I'm ready. Tonight is my first proper AA meeting offsite, and I'm bringing a new attitude with me. We load into the van and head for Maroochydore. The long drive, an hour and a half ahead of us, but there's a quiet sense of purpose in the group.

The meeting is held in a modest community room. We sit in a circle, no hiding, no back rows. There's a chairperson at a table near the front. The walls are plain, but the space feels safe. The meeting opens with a passage read from the *Big Book*, words that feel oddly familiar even though I've never heard them spoken aloud before.

Then the sharing begins.

One by one, the members speak. Their stories are raw, real. No theatrics, just truth.

Halfway through, they call my name.

This time, I don't freeze. I'm not as nervous as before. I speak. I tell them how I ended up at this rehab, I talk about how I'm feeling, how it's been hard, and how I've had to shake myself out of a slump this very morning. I don't sugarcoat it. But I don't hide, either.

And that feels good.

At the end of the meeting, the chairperson brings out a large box, it contains the sobriety chips.

This part? I've only seen it in movies.

But now it's real.

"Anyone attending their first AA meeting?"

That's me.

I stand up and walk to the front. My heart is pounding, but I'm smiling, actually smiling. I accept my chip. It's small. Simple. Just a little piece of plastic.

But to me, it's gold.

It's my first milestone. I feel something powerful rise in my chest.

Pride.

I'm doing this.

There are also a couple of rules for a successful recovery spoken about at the AA meeting: get a sponsor and DON'T get into any new relationships for at least six months, preferably twelve. (This I am totally on board with, relationships are my downfall)!!

We all pile into the bus for the long ride home. I chat with a couple of others for a while, easy conversation, light stuff, then settle back into my seat, letting the drone of the engine and the blur of headlights on the highway lull me into quiet. The darkness outside rolls by like a film, I feel at ease and I let myself breathe.

The tone is set now for the weeks ahead. I've found a rhythm, structured, familiar, strangely comforting. I follow the rules, chip away at the step work, and commit to reading the *Big Book* from cover to cover. I'm off the safety plan now, though I've been told to check in with the nurses' if I ever feel myself slipping. Fair enough.

Right now, I'm just counting down the days until Sunday, when I finally get to call my son.

The days are packed, with lessons, art therapy, and meetings. More people come and go, each with their own stories, their own quiet (and not-so-quiet) battles. It's a rotating door of humanity, raw and unfiltered. I've never felt so exposed to life, in all its mess, its beauty, its brutal honesty.

Finally, the weekend arrives. Saturday greets us with sunshine, a classic Queensland spring day. I find out we are all going on an excursion. *Woohoo.* We're heading to Rainbow Beach, a stunning stretch of coastline streaked with coloured sands, hence the name. I've never been before, and I'm buzzing with anticipation. All I can think about is diving into the ocean. I don't care how cold the water is, I need it.

We pile into the buses, voices chattering with excitement. There's even a BBQ planned. The support crew has packed eskies brimming with sausages, burger patties, bread, buns, crisp lettuce, tomatoes, onions, cheese, and every sauce imaginable. We heave them into the back and set off at 10:30 a.m., it's a forty minute drive to our destination.

The bus vibrates with energy, music playing, windows down, hair whipping in the breeze. Sunlight flashes through the trees as we head toward freedom, salt air, and sand.

When we arrive, we park up and claim a spot at the picnic area. A few people stay back to guard the eskies and snag a BBQ. The rest of us head down the stairs toward the beach.

It's even more beautiful than I imagined.

The sand shimmers in the sun, layered in ribbons of red, gold, ochre, mustard, and ash-gray, stretching along the coast like a painter's dream, blue water glistens invitingly. Cliffs of colour tower in the distance. The scent of salt air completes the picture.

I take it all in, then strip down to my swimmers and head straight for the water. The coolness hits me like a blessing. *Ohhhhhh.* Heaven. The ocean, my higher power, wraps around me, welcoming me like I've come home. I swim past the breakers, far enough to float, and let myself drift. Weightless. Free.

We swim and sunbathe for an hour then we are called back up to the picnic area for our BBQ lunch. The scent of grilled onions drifting on the breeze and the spread looks delicious. Hamburgers, sausages, warm sun and sea air, what a great day, Bellies full of food, and bodies cleansed by the ocean, we pile back into the buses and head back to the complex to wash up in time for our AA meeting this afternoon.

The next day, my second Sunday, finally comes, and with it, my chance to make a phone call. *YES!* I get to talk to my son. Not until 11:00 a.m., though. First, there are chores to be completed.

I power through mine, then race to the main reception building. I'm buzzing with nerves and hope. It's 10:40 a.m. when I get there, and there's already a small line forming outside the door. We're all desperate to hear familiar voices. I grab a chair and join the queue, heart pounding, I am so excited.

Two support workers are bringing people in for calls. My turn comes at 11:15. They lead me into reception, an open, echoing space filled with footsteps and distant conversation. There's no privacy. I'm guided to a chair. The support worker sits beside me.

"Who would you like to call?" they ask.

"My son," I say, giving them his number.

They dial, then pass me the phone, staying seated next to me to listen in. *Seriously?* This really is like jail. But I don't care. I'm going to hear my son's voice.

He answers like he's been waiting for my call. His voice is calm, familiar, grounding. He tells me that not long after I arrived here, someone from the centre contacted him. They'd arranged a Zoom call with him, Mum, and my bestie. During the call, they explained the process, what I can and can't do, how the program works, and that I'd be calling today between 11:00 a.m. and 1:00 p.m. They were also told that I can have visitors starting next Sunday, if they want to come.

I tell him I'm doing well, really well, and ask how they all are. Just hearing their voices makes my heart ache in the best and worst ways. I feel this strange mix of joy and longing, like being warmed by sunlight while standing in the rain. They can't visit, he says, not this time. But that's okay. I'll be home soon enough.

With five minutes left, I quickly ring my Mum and quickly tell her how everything is going, she sounds excited and positive for me, as always, she is there supporting me and I love her dearly for being there for me through my adult life.

And just like that, my fifteen minutes are up. The support worker gives me a gentle nod. I hand back the phone, heart still thumping with connection, and step aside for the next lucky caller.

After this, I get a surprise, *a real* surprise. My bestie has arranged to visit me, and I'm only just finding out. *What?!* This is so good.

At exactly 12:00 p.m., she arrives, picnic basket on her arm, smiling like she's smuggling in gold. She's asked to place the basket on a table so staff can check it for anything "naughty." She's already been briefed on what's allowed and what's off-limits, and she signs the visitors' register like a pro. Once she's cleared, we head up toward the hospital wing and claim a quiet picnic table.

She unpacks the basket, and oh wow, it's a mini *Patsy's Platter*! My friend is legendary for her cheese boards; they've been nicknamed "Patsy's Platters" for years. And now here I am, getting one in rehab. I feel *so* spoiled. There's also sparkling water, chilled and ready to pop. This is honestly the best surprise I could have imagined.

We sit, snack, and chat while I fill her in on how things are going here. A few of the others pass by with their own visitors, and she meets a couple of them. It feels almost normal, for a moment, like we're just two friends catching up in the sunshine. I'm having the best day. I've told her everything, what I'm experiencing here, how it's helping me, how I feel, and how certain I am that I'm going to succeed this time. Our two and a half hours vanish in what feels like minutes. Then it's time for her to go; the long road back to Brisbane waits for her. I'm blown away that she's driven two and a half hours each way just to see me for a couple of hours. My bestie, always there for me. My heart swells with love and gratitude.

Before she leaves, she says she'll be back in two weeks for another visit. I shake my head, telling her it's too far, not to put herself through the drive. But she's already nodding, insistent, her eyes sparkling with that stubborn kindness of hers. She says she'll bring one of her daughters along next time, she can drive. Oh, bless her. I'll have to fill out the paperwork to have her approved, so we set the date, another visit, another Patsy's Platter. I'm secretly thrilled.

Then, as her car pulls away, I turn back toward the main building. Rehab life resumes, swallowing me back into its rhythm.

CHAPTER TWENTY FOUR

The Funny Farm

The four times a week, three hour round trip bus rides to meetings are starting to wear thin, but I know they're doing me good. They're saying we need to hit ninety meetings in ninety days, ninety! That's intense. But by the time I leave here, I'll have racked up a solid chunk and that feels good.

Things are getting tougher inside the walls of the rehab. Not everyone gets along. Big personalities clash, some people are clearly here against their will, and more than a few are ready to throw in the towel. It's disheartening, honestly. But watching that struggle only makes my resolve stronger. I will be that one percent, the one who makes it through and stays sober.

Another favourite class of mine is nutrition. It's held once a week, and we get to cook something healthy, which I actually enjoy. The session starts with a refresher on what we *should* be eating: all the right food groups, balanced meals, the stuff most of us have been ignoring for years. Then we head to the dining room, where the ingredients are laid out like a mini cooking show. Today, we're making banana muffins, and yes, we get to eat them!

We crowd around the counter, measuring and mixing, flour dusting the air and spices scattering like confetti. It feels like we've been turned loose in the kitchen without an adult, gleeful and unrestrained. Laughter bounces off the walls, spoons clatter against bowls, and somehow the mess only adds to the fun.

When the mixture finally slides into the oven, the real magic begins. The warm scent of banana and cinnamon drifts through the dining room, curling around us, tugging at our appetites until our mouths water. I can't help but grin, knowing I've tucked away one of my precious coffee sachets for a moment just like this. Soon, I'll have a steaming mug in hand, washing down a muffin in proper style.

Saturday rolls around again, and this week's excursion takes us to the local Pizza Hut. All you can eat? Yes please! We pile onto the buses like kids on a school trip, buzzing with restless energy. As the engines rumble to life and we roll out of the car park, I can't help but laugh. It feels like something straight out of *Funny Farm*, a ragtag bunch of misfits hijacking a bus and joyriding through town. That's us: a busload of loonies, hungry for carbs and a taste of freedom.

When we arrive, we tumble off the buses like animals starved for days. I almost feel sorry for the poor souls inside, hoping for a quiet lunch. They don't know what's about to hit them, the local institute crew, unleashed and ravenous.

The support workers herd us into line, asking us to file in neatly and respectfully, and, miracle of miracles, we do.

The moment we step inside, the smell hits me. Warm, yeasty crust, melted cheese, a dozen different toppings blending into one heavenly perfume. I'm in food paradise. We take over half the restaurant, plastic cups already set out on tables, pitchers of soft drink standing by to quench our thirst.

I'm among the first at the pizza bar, plate in hand, stacking slices like a champion, one of everything, just to be safe. Each bite is glorious, salty, gooey, hot. When I've demolished the first round, I make a token visit to the salad bar, just enough to pretend I'm balancing things out.

But who am I kidding? I'm really saving room for the crown jewel: the dessert bar.

With our bellies stretched and our energy spent, we're herded back onto the buses and carted home to the farm. The ride feels slower this time, everyone slouched in their seats, lulled into silence by food comas and fizzy drinks.

As soon as we arrive, I make a beeline for my room. I flop down, content to let that glorious feast settle, the taste of pizza and soft serve still lingering. The afternoon drifts by in a haze of comfort and drowsy satisfaction, a calm before the evening ahead. Soon enough, it'll be time to pull myself together and head out again for the AA meeting.

Finally it's Sunday, phone call day. I power through my rostered chores, every sweep, wipe, and tidy charged with purpose. My heart quickens as I head to the main building, today I'm first in line. They call me through, they dial my son. We talk for ten precious minutes, even passing the phone around so I can say hello to the rest of the family. As the seconds slip away, I squeeze in a quick call to Mum.

I tell them all I'm doing well, that the meetings seem endless but are slowly helping me untangle the knots in my head. We sign off for another week, their voices still echoing in my mind as I wander outside. The sun is warm against my skin, and I sink into it, letting the light spill over me while I find a hidden space to go and tackle my homework.

One and a half weeks to go. The home stretch, well, sort of. Ten days. Saying it out loud makes it feel like forever. Lessons, meetings, dramas, people arriving with hope or leaving in disgrace, it's a constant tide. And the rules here are no joke. Break one, and you're out. I've seen it happen. I can't wait to leave this behind, to focus on myself, to stitch my life back together.

I power through the week, same routine as the previous three weeks, I've got this down pat. Then, the last Sunday arrives. No Saturday outing for the "funny farm" patients this week, which is a disappointment, but apparently we only get that escape three Saturdays out of four. No matter. Today is going to be a great day. I can feel it in my bones. Last time I have to line up for the phone calls with my son, my family, my Mum, and then, a visit. Yes.

My bestie arrives with her daughter, their arms full of a picnic basket that gets searched for any 'naughty stuff'. They sign the visitors' log, pens scratching against the paper, and we head out to claim a picnic table. The afternoon air smells faintly of cut grass, and the sunlight flickers through gum leaves. She lays out her famous platter, cheeses, crackers, fresh fruit glistening in the light, sparkling water poured into plastic cups and we settle in.

We talk non-stop for two and a half hours. Friends I've made here drift over, curious. They've heard about my bestie and her platters and want to meet her themselves. Laughter and chatter ripple around us, the air thick with warmth and connection.

Then she looks at me and says, "Jane, you're in the wrong profession."

I blink. "Why?"

She gestures around us. "Just look. People are drawn to you. They listen. They respect you. You're meant to help people like you."

"No way," I say, shaking my head. "I can't do that. I don't have that in me, I'm struggling to help myself."

But her words linger in the air, another seed is planted…

Three days to go. I'm leaving on Wednesday, and I can't wait. My bags are already packed, anticipation buzzing through me, though a thin thread of dread lies beneath it. The big, bad world is out there, waiting. But this time will be different. I'll do the ninety in ninety. I'll ask for help. I'll find a sponsor. I will not get into any new relationships. I will succeed.

My cake day has finally arrived, it's my last day in rehab, and I'm going home. I walk into the room and take my place at the front. There's no family here for me, but Mr. Rugged, the gem of a man who's been patiently teaching us the basics, sits beside me as my representative. His steady presence feels like enough.

Kind words and well-wishes are spoken, and I accept them with genuine gratitude. This place has given me so much, though it's an experience I sincerely hope never to repeat. Intense doesn't even begin to cover it.

When my ride pulls up, I step outside, heart light and restless. The car carries me back down the highway toward Brisbane, the road unfurling ahead like a promise. Another ending, yes, but more importantly, another new beginning.

The Recovery

CHAPTER TWENTY FIVE

Life After the Fourth Rehab – Sobriety Take Four

Home from rehab, I unpack slowly, setting each thing in its place as if I'm reassembling my life piece by piece. The air in my apartment smells faintly of dust and laundry detergent, home, imperfect but mine.

Now the hard work begins. I have to get this right. This is my last chance at sobriety, and I can feel the weight of that truth pressing against my ribs. I download the AA and NA apps, their blue-and-white icons glowing like lifelines on my phone. The lists appear, meetings, times, places, and I trace my finger down the screen, searching for the ones closest to me.

I draft a schedule, one meeting every day. Today is Wednesday, so tonight I'll log into the Zoom meeting hosted back at the rehab. I type it into my calendar as a standing appointment, every Wednesday, without fail. I fill in the rest of the week: Thursday, AA at Mt Gravatt. Friday, NA at New Farm. Saturday, NA at Alexandra Hills. Sunday, AA at Wynnum or Coorporoo. Monday, AA at Gumdale. Tuesday, AA again at Wynnum. The list looks solid, dependable, like a scaffold I can cling to until my footing feels steadier.

When evening comes, I open Zoom. The screen floods with familiar faces, and my chest warms. It's only been hours since I left, but seeing them again feels like slipping into a favourite sweater. They smile when they see me, and the sound of their voices through my laptop speakers is almost enough to make me forget I'm sitting alone in my lounge room.

After the meeting, I stay on to chat with a couple of close friends. I tell them I'm doing great, genuinely glad to be home. They still have two more months to go, but when they move to the halfway house, they'll be just a short drive away. Knowing that makes the night feel a little less lonely.

Now that I'm home, I slip back into my routine, no mucking around. I want life to settle into a new normal as soon as possible.

The next morning, I head into work, my desk exactly as I left it, a neat little time capsule of unfinished tasks. I dive in, catching up on everything I had to put on hold for rehab. The rhythm feels good, the tapping of keys, the shuffle of papers, I'm back.

I am looking forward to tonight, I'm attending my first meeting on my own. The thought churns in my stomach, equal parts dread and determination. I know I'll get through it.

I drive to Mt Gravatt, the headlights cutting through the darkness. The meeting is at a church, its pale brick walls rise up against the night sky, looming like something ancient and watchful. I park on the street, my heart thudding so hard I can feel it in my throat.

The air is cool and still as I walk toward the building, scanning for a sign. Then I see it: a white placard glowing in the dark, bold black letters reading *AA Meeting*. Relief washes through me. I follow the narrow path down the side of the church, into what looks like a basement storeroom.

Inside, the air smells faintly of dust and old carpet. Benches line the walls, mismatched chairs scattered here and there. At the front, a table is set with AA banners hanging behind it. I choose a chair not too far from the front, trying to look calm, though I feel like a deer caught in headlights.

Then, luck. A young girl walks in, and I know her. She was at rehab with me, now in the halfway house. I stand and wrap her in a warm hug. The knot in my chest loosens. I'm not alone anymore. My confidence rises, I've got this.

The meeting begins, voices filling the room in a familiar rhythm. Halfway through, someone calls on me to introduce myself. My pulse quickens, but I stand and speak, just a quick story about how I ended up here, how new I am to all of this. They listen, smiling, nodding, making space for me.

By the time I sit down, I realize my shoulders have unclenched. That wasn't so bad. Rehab didn't just help me get sober, it trained me for this. And tonight, I feel grateful for that.

The next night, I head to the NA meeting at New Farm. This one's in a community centre, a bright, airy two-story complex. The meeting room sits on the ground floor, spacious and hushed, giving off library vibes. I step inside alone, heart thudding, nerves on high alert. The place is full, at least thirty people. Chairs line the walls in an oval, and I slip into an empty one, landing with an ungraceful plonk. The uncertainty creeps back in.

I scan the room and spot a familiar face, one of the long-termers from the halfway house I met during rehab. I smile, wave. My shoulders drop a little.

The meeting begins. It's a clean-living theme. A book makes its way around the circle, each person reading a passage if they feel moved, then sharing their thoughts. When it reaches me, someone asks if I'd like to read. I do. *Jump in with both feet,* I tell myself. The words leave my mouth steadier than I expect. I share. I finish. I thank them. Relief washes over me as I sit back. Another meeting conquered.

Saturday brings another NA meeting, this one in Alexandra Hills, inside the main part of a church. Teak pews stretch out in rows, their bright red upholstery dotted with colourful cushions. Above, a raked wooden ceiling glows warm under soft light. The atmosphere feels almost sacred.

I walk in with more confidence this time. At the front, a lovely young woman greets me, bubbly, bright, the kind of warmth you feel instantly. She shows me the kitchen, points out the tea, coffee, and biscuits.

When I return to the meeting area, a man who looks like he just stepped out of a rock band, welcomes me with a wide grin and a firm handshake. My guard drops completely. I slide into one of the pews. The room is filling up, a hum of voices beneath the high ceiling.

The meeting begins. I'm asked to share, and I tell my story, how I became who I am now. I also have the confidence to share exactly how I am feeling, I say, I really wanted a drink today. I was driving here, thinking how I would love to just go home, drink wine until I'm drunk and listen to very loud music, just like I used to do every night. But I didn't turn the car around, I kept driving here, and now that urge is gone.

I see them all nodding their heads like they totally get it, and that's because they do, they relate to exactly what I am saying and that makes me feel amazing, I am not the only one, these are my people and I couldn't be happier. I listen to the others, their words settle in me like echoes, each one a reminder of the storms we've weathered and the strength it's taken to survive.

Sunday. An AA meeting in Coorparoo, 10:00 a.m., under the shade of a sprawling tree in the local park. The morning air is fresh, carrying the scent of cut grass and damp earth. I spot the group, fifteen or so people in a loose circle of plastic chairs. I pull one up, the legs sinking slightly into the soft ground, and join in. The meeting flows: greetings, formalities, shares. Then it's over. Simple. Easy. The rest of the day is mine. I stretch out at home, letting exhaustion wash over me and I sleep.

Monday. Another AA meeting, this time at Gumdale. The gathering takes place in an old-style hall, weatherboard walls, polished timber

floors that creak underfoot, a small kitchen tucked out the back, and a stage set at the front. Bench seats are arranged in a wide circle around the chairperson's table, draped neatly with AA banners.

When I arrive, about half a dozen people are already there, chatting quietly, the room carrying that mix of nerves and comfort that these meetings always seem to hold. I take a seat on one of the benches, and soon enough the meeting begins. Once again, I'm asked to share. I introduce myself and give a short account of the past few weeks, and as always, I feel that warmth, welcomed, accepted, folded back into the family I didn't know I needed.

Tuesday. AA at Wynnum. The meeting is in an old Queenslander-style community hall, the kind with weatherboard walls and wide verandas. Ours is under the main building, a bright, airy room. Chairs form a neat circle; a table stands at the front with the AA banners draped across it.

I'm barely through the door when a bubbly young woman greets me, her smile genuine. She introduces herself and gives me the lay of the land. Another woman catches my eye, warm, approachable. I take the seat next to her. We chat quietly, small talk but friendly, until the meeting begins.

When it ends, she turns to me, slips a piece of paper into my hand. Her phone number. "Call me if you need anything, or just to talk."

I'm floored, just like I was all those years ago back in Yeppoon. The gesture lands deep, past the part of me that's used to doing this alone. I thank her, and step out into the moonlight. On the walk to my car, a thought takes hold: *Could she be a sponsor? Would she sponsor me?* I decide to sit with the idea for a few days.

Wednesday. A week back home. A meeting every day. I've learned about a few others nearby and I'm itching to try them. The fatigue hits hard now, the bone-deep kind I know as recovery fatigue. But I know how to handle it this time. I get home from work, collapse into a twenty-minute power nap, and wake just in time to get ready for the evening's meeting. It's a rhythm now. A routine.

Thursday night, I try an NA meeting in Wynnum, held in a community hall not far from the calming waters of Moreton Bay. I find a park and walk toward the pale-brick building. Outside, clusters of people laugh and chat, cigarette smoke curling into the cool night air.

One of the ladies walks up and introduces herself, I immediately feel a connection with her, she will be a good friend, I just know it. Inside, a wide circle of chairs surrounds a central table, NA banners draped proudly along the wall. I take a seat and watch the room fill, forty people, maybe more. A fantastic turnout. I listen intently to all of the speakers and I am filled with hope as I am at every meeting.

The following Tuesday night I am back at the Wynnum AA meeting and I pluck up the courage to ask the lady who gave me her number to be my sponsor, she says YES. I am gobsmacked, I feel so privileged she is willing to help me navigate the twelve steps. We arrange some times to meet over the next few weeks, everything is falling into place.

CHAPTER TWENTY SIX

Racing and Rebuilding

Three weeks out of rehab, and I'm already at my first major motorsport event, the famous Noosa Hill Climb. Three days of racing through the hinterland outside Noosa, a lush rainforest where the road snakes its way to the top of the range. Normally open to the public, this strip of winding asphalt is closed for the weekend, with grandstands set up for spectators to watch us charge to the summit.

Friday morning, a few of us from the club meet north of Brisbane and convoy up the highway together. It feels like a road trip, all camaraderie and anticipation, but there's one problem. Rain. Not just a passing shower. A monsoon has parked itself over the coast, and it's going nowhere. For three days, it's us, the hill, and a wall of water.

We roll through the gates and find our spot, then set up camp. The BMW Club marquee goes up in the downpour, livery snapping against the wind, rain dripping from our noses and soaking us to the skin. But spirits are high, nothing can wash away the thrill of being here. We register, stick our numbers and secure our timing gear to our cars. Suddenly, I feel it in my chest: I'm not a spectator, I'm not pretending, this is professional, and I'm a competitor.

That afternoon we have a practice run to get our bearings. No racing yet, just feeling out the course, learning the curves and searching for the all-important racing line. Even at a steady pace, the road feels alive: slick, narrow, twisting like a snake through dripping green forest.

Later, I check into a nearby resort, drop my bags, and dress up for the drivers' dinner. The rain keeps most people away, but a few of us gather, and I spend the night grilling experienced drivers with questions. Every tip feels like gold.

Saturday dawns even wetter than Friday. Sheets of rain hammer the track. I tell myself, *Be cautious, take it easy.* At sign-on, my car passes scrutineering, and with 115 entries all up which is actually down because of the rain, the day feels enormous. I'm number ninety-two, plenty of time to watch the others take off, note their speeds, their approaches to those first tricky turns.

And then, it's me. Race gear on. Helmet strapped tight. Sports mode engaged. I inch toward the start line, heart thudding. The marshal waves me forward. I take a long breath, eyes fixed on the light. It snaps green, GO.

The tyres bite hard, water spraying in twin plumes. The wipers thrash double time as I brake gently for the first corner, sliding through clean. My girl's rear end kicks just slightly, perfect, controlled and exhilarating. Corner after corner, I'm threading her up the mountain, dancing in the rain, adrenaline flooding every nerve. In a flash, the finish line looms, I punch across it, breathless. *Oh my God. What a feeling.* My grin hurts, my hands shake, and I'm buzzing, utterly alive.

At the muster line, cars queue to head back down the hill at parade pace. I leap out into the torrential rain, spot my pink-haired teammate, and throw my arms around her in the biggest, soggiest bear hug. She's the one who encouraged me to try this, and I couldn't be more grateful.

Second run. I'm hungry now. Determined. Still raining, still slick, but I'm leaning harder, braver, faster. The car slides like she was born for these bends, and I *know* before I even see the clock, I've beaten my time.

Between runs, we huddle under the marquee, shivering and muddy. The paddock has turned into a swamp, boots sinking into the muck with every step. No matter, we're laughing, soaked to the bone and I am loving every moment of it.

By mid-afternoon the officials call it. Too wet, too dangerous, racing suspended. Three runs in the bag, and I don't care that the day's been cut short. I've just raced the Noosa Hill Climb, in a monsoon. What an experience.

Because the racing wraps early, I decide to head north to Gympie for the AA meeting starting at 4:30. Some of my friends from rehab will be there, and it's only an hour away. I want to see how they're doing.

I drive through the downpour, wipers thrashing, headlights carving through the gray curtain of rain. The smell of damp leather and lingering gasoline fills the car. I pull into the lot just in time, the rain easing as if to let me out.

Inside the meeting hall, it's warm, dry, and familiar. The smell of instant coffee and biscuits lingers in the air. My friends are there, faces I've sweated through rehab with, and it's a rush of relief to see them smiling, steady, still here. We catch up quickly before the meeting starts. Everyone's doing well.

When I'm asked to share, I stand and speak from the gut: how I've been going to a meeting every day, how much it keeps me on track, and, this is the big one, that I'm actually racing this weekend. Heads nod, some smiles break out. My chest swells. For a moment, it feels like two worlds, recovery and racing, are threading together into something solid.

As soon as the meeting ends, I have to dash, back into the wet night, back toward Noosa for the team dinner. I slide into the restaurant just in time, still damp, still buzzing. My teammates are already gathered, laughing over meals, swapping stories. I sit down, tired but glowing. What a day.

Sunday dawns with no dawn at all, just the same low ceiling of monsoonal rain, hammering down with no mercy. The air is thick and wet, smelling of soaked asphalt and dripping gum trees.

I get to the track early, eager for the first run. Fewer drivers today, the weather has scared some off, which means quicker turnarounds for those of us still standing. My number is called, and I fire up the car, grinning despite the sheets of rain.

The launch is just as exhilarating as yesterday. My girl grips, slides, corrects, and surges. Every corner feels like a battle and a dance at the same time. By the top, my pulse is pounding, and I'm already planning how I'll take the line differently next time. I know it in my bones, I'll be back for this event.

One more run and then, halt! At mid morning the officials call it. Not the rain this time, but something worse: one of the open-wheelers has blown a sump and spilled oil all over the course. With the downpour, there's no way to clean it up. Racing is over. Damn.

We pack down the marquee in the mud, fold dripping canvas, load our filthy cars, and trade hugs and farewells. The track empties, the forest swallowing the noise again. I roll back onto the highway toward Brisbane.

And just like that, the rain stops. The sky clears, streaks of late sun cutting across the road. I laugh out loud in the car. You've got to be kidding me.

This weekend, I'll never forget it.

The weeks blur into a rhythm, work, meetings and sleep. Each day folds into the next, but within the sameness there's a thread of hope. My sponsor, patient and wise, sits with me once a week as we read through the AA book together. Her voice carries the weight of experience, grounding me as I trace the words on the page. We don't just skim; we talk, unraveling the steps until they make sense in my bones. This is nothing like filling out answers in a workbook. It's alive, spoken and shared. I hold myself accountable, not with empty promises but with honesty, with the sting of admitting where I've gone wrong, and the relief that follows when the truth finally has air.

Then comes a milestone: sixty days sober. At AA I'm presented with a chip from my sponsor, cool and solid in my palm. At NA, a key tag, light but no less meaningful. Two small tokens, two great meetings. I'm proud, really proud. Still sober. Still showing up every day. Still building a life that feels like mine again. I am winning.

On the track, life keeps pace. I compete in a couple of Khanacross events, weaving through slaloms of traffic cones, pushing the car fast but clean, careful not to clip a single one. The rush of precision driving is its own reward, but the year saves one more gift for me.

As 2022 winds down, I'm called up at the BMWCQ presentation lunch and awarded the club's first ever, Motorsport Encouragement Award. The applause, the weight of the plaque in my hands, the recognition from my peers, it all lands deep. Recovery, racing and rebuilding: it's all happening.

What does life have installed for me next?…

CHAPTER TWENTY SEVEN

Gypsy Jane

January 2023, another adventure begins, a five-day, round-trip cruise on the majestic *Queen Mary II*, sailing from Sydney to Burnie, Tasmania, with my trusty travel companion, my beautiful Mum. I booked this voyage back in early 2022, in the middle of my last relapse, unsure if I would ever be sober again. Now, to my absolute delight, I am, five months sober, to be exact.

I fly into Sydney the day before departure, while Mum jets in from Launceston. We've planned it this way so there's no risk of travel delays spoiling our boarding day. We meet at the airport, all smiles and suitcases, then hop on the train to Darling Harbour for an overnight stay.

Sailing day. We arrive at Circular Quay, the tang of saltwater in the breeze, eager to board this regal vessel, she towers above the wharf, her dark hull and crimson funnel a regal silhouette against the bright Sydney sky. This is no ordinary cruise, it's the inaugural Culinary Cruise, with three renowned Australian guest chefs on board to dazzle us with their creations. The check-in process is brisk; we're handed our swipe cards to our cabin and to onboard indulgences, and then we step onto the polished decks of the Queen.

Our cabin is classic cruise-ship style: two neat single beds dressed in crisp white linens, a compact bathroom, a desk with a single chair, a balcony that smells faintly of sea spray, and a mini fridge perfect for keeping my cold water. We unpack quickly before exploring the duty-free shops, glimmering lounges and quiet libraries. By late afternoon we're on the top deck for the sail-away party. At exactly 4:00 p.m., the ship's horn booms deep and low, vibrating through my chest. The Harbour Bridge and Opera House drift into the distance, slipping away like a scene in a movie. Next stop: Melbourne.

That night we dine in the buffet, where the air is thick with aromas, roasted meats, steamed vegetables, fresh bread still warm from the oven. I pile my plate high. After dinner, I sneak a few small desserts back to our room, tucking them in the fridge for later. A hot chocolate will be the perfect companion. I end the night walking the upper decks, the sea stretched out in every direction, the scent of salt sharp in the cool night air. The ocean, my higher power, feels infinite, deep blue, powerful, and calming.

The next morning is a full day at sea. After breakfast, I study the daily onboard schedule, scanning for the Alcoholics Anonymous (AA) meeting. It's listed under "Friends of Bill W." (after Bill Wilson who wrote the AA Book) at 4:30 p.m, the witching hour for me, perfect. Also listed are the times the guest chefs will be showcasing their culinary delights, so I pencil them into my lazy day schedule. In between, I explore the ship's many levels, then sink into a sun lounge by the pool, soaking in the sunshine and breathing in the mingled scent of sunscreen and salt air.

At 4:30 sharp, I arrive at the designated meeting room on Deck 10. The space is unexpectedly beautiful, plush leather chairs, vintage lamps casting warm light, low coffee tables, and a panoramic view of the endless ocean. What a stunning place to share and be heard. Only two others are in the room. One is an entertainer on board, I had seen him performing the night before, he is traveling the world for six months with his guitar, and his son, who plays alongside him.

The other explains he is cruising with his wife on what he casually calls their "umpteenth" voyage.

We begin. The entertainer opens his worn copy of the AA *Big Book*, and we hold a traditional meeting. We talk, we listen, we laugh softly. There's no judgment here, only the quiet recognition of what we share and the long, hard road that brought us here. Sitting in that sunlit room, the ocean rolling endlessly beyond the glass, I feel humbled. Who would have thought, me, here, telling my story in this glorious setting, and having others nod in understanding.

Our third day, we dock in Melbourne under a sky washed clean by morning light. My cousin is waiting at the cruise terminal, waving enthusiastically before whisking us away in her car. The salty tang of the docks fades as we merge into the city's bustle. She's taking us to the Monet exhibition at the convention centre, a visual feast where his famous works are projected onto towering walls and sculptural displays.

The room glows in shifting hues: lilac water lilies, gold-dusted haystacks, the soft blues of dawn. The paintings ripple and flow across the surfaces as if the walls themselves are breathing. It feels like standing inside Monet's mind. Afterward, we linger over a divine lunch at the centre's restaurant, al dente pasta, warm bread, and the delicate perfume of citrus in my dish making me close my eyes in contentment.

By late afternoon we're back at the terminal, hugging our farewells before we step back on board. My meeting calls. The three of us gather again, speaking the language only we understand, the shorthand of survival, struggle, and quiet triumph. I leave feeling grounded, blessed to be here, sober, and living this life.

The next morning we dock in Burnie. It's a flawless February day, the kind where the sky is a clear, unbroken blue and the air holds just enough chill to feel crisp against your skin. From the deck, I breathe in the scent of eucalyptus drifting from the hills and think, *I could live here.*

We join a tour through the region's canyons and caves, where the cool, earthy smell of damp stone mingles with the sweet scent of wildflowers. Sunlight filters through leaves, dappling the ground like an impressionist painting. It's a day filled with breathtaking scenery, each turn in the path revealing another postcard-perfect view. I think this place is truly beautiful, could I possibly…move?

The rest of the cruise is a slow, indulgent journey back to Sydney. My days blur into a rhythm of sunbathing, swimming, and savoring every culinary offering the chefs present. This inaugural Culinary Cruise is a parade of flavors, delicate pastries dusted with sugar, glossy chocolate tarts, tangy lemon slices that make my mouth water. I attend every cooking demonstration, watching skilled hands transform simple ingredients into edible art.

Sweet treats are the crown jewels of my days now, no longer numbing myself with alcohol, I savor each bite, each texture, each burst of flavor. And as the Queen Mary II slices through the glittering water, I know I'm tasting life itself.

Back in Brisbane, the humid air wraps around me like a damp blanket. I now have a decision to make, my lease ends in April, and the thought has been simmering for months, find somewhere cheaper. I've been here nearly a year, and after the wreckage of my last relationship, living alone in a three-story, three-bedroom townhouse has become a financial weight I can't keep carrying.

But something else has been stirring since the cruise—-Tasmania. That crisp air still lingers in my mind. Could I really do it? I hate the cold. Always have. But the move would untangle so many of my problems in one bold step.

I feel that old danger creeping in, lost, hollow, teetering on the edge of a spiral I might not climb out of. I do not want another relapse on my hands. The more I think about Tasmania, the more it glows like a lighthouse through my fog. Mum is turning eighty-one, living alone, and she's been saying for two years now, *You could move here, you know!* I can still hear the lilt in her voice when she says it, half hopeful, half daring me.

I've visited often over the years. I know the streets, the scent of woodsmoke in winter, the way the sun sets over stunning beaches. I do love the place. But the question churns in my head day and night: *What do I do? I ask the universe!*

It doesn't take me too long to decide. This move will help me financially, I am living day to day, spending all of my wage on rent and utilities. I speak to my manager about my decision. He's surprised, how could he not be? But he's also deeply supportive. He knows exactly what I've been through, and he's one of the biggest reasons I've stayed steady in my recovery. We discuss the possibility of a job transfer; after all, the company has a depot in Tasmania. But the nearest one is a hundred kilometers from where I'd be living, and it turns out the depot isn't busy enough to need extra staff. That door closes quietly, and I remind myself to trust the universe, if not this path, then another will open.

A few days later, I meet up with my old flatmate for lunch. I tell him of my decision and he totally agrees, this is what I need to do. Afterward, we wander the streets, and I spot a table of books outside a shop. Sitting right on top is a 2023 Gratitude Diary, its cover warm and inviting. "This is exactly what I need," I say, and he buys it for me, a birthday gift.

It turns out to be more than just a diary. Each month begins with a short reflection, stories, facts, suggestions for living with intention. One entry introduces me to the High Heart, the eighth chakra, the center of unconditional love and spiritual purpose. As I read, I feel something inside me shift. My heart feels lighter, my mind clearer. I have another purpose now, this one I can only find by stepping into this new life.

When I talk to my son, daughter-in-law, and grandchildren about moving to Tasmania, they're fully supportive. They've walked this nine-year sobriety journey alongside me, cheering me on through every stumble and triumph. I know I'll miss them terribly, but to be the best mother and grandmother I can, I need to care for myself first. And my Mum, well, she's over the moon I am coming down to live. I can hear the joy in her voice over the phone when I tell her.

With the blessing of my family on both sides of the Bass Strait, I begin putting my plan into action. The future, once hazy, now feels like a map unfolding in front of me.

I start scanning the job market in Tasmania, sending off applications to anything that feels like a good fit. Then one listing catches my eye, it's similar to what I do now, at a workplace not far from where I'll be living. My heart leaps. I can already picture myself walking through their doors, making a difference, contributing something meaningful.

Within days, I have interviews lined up for three different roles, but that one remains my focus. I feel certain about it, so certain that I ask the universe outright: *Let this be the one.*

Ask and you shall receive. The magic works. Two offers come in, and I take the one I had my heart set on.

With my future officially in motion, I set an end date at my current job, a start date at my new one, and turn my attention to shedding the life I've built here. My rule is simple: if it doesn't fit in my car, it doesn't come with me. This is a clean break, a fresh start.

Over the next six weeks, my townhouse transforms into a staging ground of goodbyes, furniture leaving through the front door in the arms of strangers, bags of clothes dropped off at charity shops, little treasures handed to friends. Some items are hard to let go of, but each time I do, I feel lighter.

Finally, the day comes. I pack my baby girl, my convertible, every inch carefully filled with the essentials for my new life. I am starting from scratch once again, the possessions in my car are everything I own. The sun is hot on my shoulders as I close the boot, take one last look at the townhouse, and slide behind the wheel.

09th May 2023, the road to Melbourne unfurls ahead of me, a ribbon of possibility. When I drive onto the *Spirit of Tasmania*, the scent of salt and diesel fills the air. My car, my possessions, and I will cross the Bass Strait together. As the ship pulls away, the mainland drifts into the distance, and I feel it in my bones, this is the start of the best chapter of my life.

The move is behind me, the boxes unpacked, and my new job already feels like a natural fit. Weekends are my time to roam, jumping in the car and driving from coast to coast, soaking up scenery so beautiful it almost feels unreal. The rolling green hills, the misty mountain ranges, the sudden sparkle of water when you crest a hill and see the ocean stretched out before you. They say Tasmania has the cleanest air in the world, and from what I breathe in here, crisp, cool, carrying the faint scent of the ocean I believe it.

I look up the local AA and NA meetings in Tasmania and find them not far from home, right in the center of Launceston. AA is running every night of the week, while NA meets on Sundays and Wednesdays. Sundays are double days: AA at 2:00 p.m., then NA at 5:00 p.m.

That first Sunday, I head in for both. The meetings are held in a room tucked behind a grand old church in the heart of town, stone towers, stained-glass windows glowing faintly even on a gray day. The place must be over a century old, solid and solemn.

Inside, the meeting room is mercifully warm. Bar heaters line the walls, glowing red and blasting heat against the chill that seeps in from outside. It's bitterly cold out there, the kind of cold that bites your skin and lingers in your bones, so the warmth inside feels like a relief.

Each meeting is small, just a handful of people gathered in the circle. I share at both, but something feels off. I can't quite settle. Maybe it's the cold, maybe just the different atmosphere here, it puts me on edge.

Still, I remind myself: I'll try again. Sometimes it takes more than one go to feel at home.

I've already joined a racing club before arriving in Tasmania, determined to keep competing in motorsport.

July 2023. I'm competing in my first motorkhana being held at Symmons Plains Raceway. The winter air bites at my cheeks, sharp and damp. It's a typical Tasmanian winter's day, overcast skies pressing low, drizzle needling my skin, and a cold that seeps into my bones. The scent of petrol and warm rubber hangs thick in the air, promising speed.

My baby girl, purrs beneath me, eager, twitching like she knows the cones ahead are our prey. This should be interesting, considering I'm right–left dyslexic and have to follow precise directions around those very cones.

I roll into position for my first run, creep to the start line, and, GO. I slam the accelerator, the rear tyres biting into the wet surface. I throw her into each turn, tyres screeching, engine roaring, spray fanning out behind us. The course blurs at the edges. Adrenaline surges through me, hot and electric, my grin stretching so wide my cheeks ache. I'm fairly sure I took the right turns at every intersection… fairly sure.

Three more runs follow, each one tougher than the last. The damp track glistens, the cones seem to multiply, and my dyslexic brain works overtime. But with every pass, my confidence grows. I push harder, brake later, steer faster, the girl and I are flying now.

Earlier, I'd wandered through the clubhouse and seen the trophies displayed on a table, each one polished to a mirror shine. I thought, *I want to win one of those. Imagine how great that would be.*

The day wraps up. We crowd into the clubhouse, damp jackets steaming in the warmth. My hair is plastered to my cheeks, my hands still tingling from the steering wheel. The announcer starts with third place. Not me. Second place. Still not me. I smile, tell myself, *Better luck next time, I must have taken some wrong turns after all.*

Then—"First place, Ladies category… Jane Musgrave!"

The words seem to hang in the air for a heartbeat, suspended in disbelief. My name. My name. The room erupts, but the sound hits me in muffled waves. My legs go light. I walk up in a daze, each step landing like it belongs to someone else. Then the trophy is in my hands, solid, cold, dazzling in the light, and it's real.

Eleven months ago, I couldn't have imagined this moment. Now, it's mine.

My next big milestone: I buy another car. When I moved, I had no intention of doing so, but that's how my life unfolds, nothing planned, everything just happening. My beloved convertible, my baby girl, is getting old and having a few issues. I decide to buy a brand new one because it will have the manufacturer's warranty. So by the end of July, I welcome a new addition to my family: a BMW 128Ti hot hatch. Sleek, fast, and unapologetically built for racing, I christen her *Stella*.

She's skyscraper grey with sharp red accents, calipers that pop, stitching that gleams, and black leather sport seats that hug me in tight. Every feature sings BMW, right down to the heated steering wheel, a true blessing in Tasmania's cold. The first time I slide behind the wheel, I know, Stella and I are going to be trouble. And with a sprint day at Symmons Plains Raceway marked on the calendar for October, I can't wait to unleash her on the track.

CHAPTER TWENTY EIGHT

Finding my Gift

As my new life takes shape, I decide to try pet and house sitting. It's a way to explore more of the island and, if I'm honest, to give Mum and me a little breathing room. We love each other dearly, but after years of living alone, we've both grown used to our own rhythms.

It turns out to be one of the best decisions I've ever made. I sign up to a couple of house-sitting sites and start booking jobs right away. Another plus of now being a non-drinker is I can put this on my profile for the sitting sites with total honesty, having this in my corner helps me secure the sits that I apply for.

One listing in particular catches my heart, a home in a seaside town north of Launceston, they are looking for someone urgently to look after their adorable cat, Pixie, I immediately reach out to them. I've always dreamed of living by the beach again, but I never thought it could happen in Tasmania. And yet, here I am. Helping someone out and fulfilling a dream!

The three-week sit turns into three months. The house is perched on a grassy hill above the beautiful village called Beechford, with views of the ocean from one side and the mountains from the other. The salty breeze becomes my morning alarm, and my evening walks are spent with waves curling at my feet and the sky shifting through every shade of gold and pink. The locals welcome me like an old friend, and soon I'm booked for three more sits in the same community. This never would have been possible if I were still drinking. I've achieved my dream of living at the beach again, and it's exactly as healing as I'd hoped. The ocean is my sanctuary.

I don't go back to the AA or NA meetings here. They're too far from me now, and to be honest, the cold night air cuts straight through me, making the idea unbearable. I tell myself I'm living the dream now, and in many ways, I am, but the truth is, the struggles of an addict don't just vanish. Some days the craving rises sharp and sudden, like a tide pulling at my feet, and I have to talk myself down. I've gotten good at riding that wave, steadying myself against its pull. Years of practice have taught me that I can't test my limits. Sobriety isn't just for today or tomorrow. It's for life.

I cope with being so far from my AA and NA peers by holding them close in thought. On Thursday nights, when the clock strikes seven, I picture the Wynnum meeting beginning. I imagine the circle of chairs, the scrape of someone pulling one forward, the shuffle of feet as people settle in. I see the faces I know so well, some tired, some glowing, all carrying the same unspoken understanding.

I sit quietly, letting myself be there in spirit. I breathe in, and it feels like I'm inhaling their presence, that collective strength that once kept me afloat when I couldn't do it alone. I let their love and support wrap around me like a blanket, warm and familiar, even though I'm miles away.

October 14 arrives: super sprint day. I drive out to Symmons Plains and the cold hits me straight away, freezing wind, low clouds, we even have sleet today! I prepare Stella and line up for scrutineering, nerves buzzing. This is my first time racing on the main track here. I don't know anyone, and since I have moved here, I feel genuinely alone. Out of thirty-four drivers, I'm the only female on the grid.

Relief comes when a few familiar faces from the club recognize me. They wave me over and invite me to join their team, four drivers required for each run. I'm grateful, and we quickly set our running order. I happily take the back spot. New track, new car, better to learn before leading.

Once we're out there, though, it all clicks. The car feels alive beneath me, surging forward with each gear, every curve a test, every straight a thrill. I push her as far as I dare for a first outing, and on the back straight I hit 197 kph. The adrenaline is pure fire.

We have four runs for each class and for the last race I have worked my way up to start in the coveted pole position on the starting grid. The thrill of racing, the thrill of driving like this when I have never done any formal training before, blows me away. By the end of the day, I'm glowing. Stella and I have posted the best times in our vehicle class. I'm proud, beyond proud. This is what I came here for.

That sprint day at Symmons Plains turns out to be my last event in Tasmania, but what a way to finish.

But with this newfound happiness, comes a familiar restlessness. I start to wonder, *What now? Why am I really here? What's my purpose?* The questions sit heavy in my chest until, not long after, the answer finds me.

In late October, a man I follow on social media, formerly known as the Famous Flower Man, announces something that sparks through me like a firecracker: he's running a course called *Unleash Your Manifesting Genie*. I've always believed in manifesting; I've seen it unfold too many times in my own life to dismiss it. The course will be held over four nights in November, via Zoom. I sign up instantly, my heart thumping with a mix of curiosity and certainty.

Three weeks later, it's time. Twenty-nine of us appear in our little glowing squares on the screen, strangers yet somehow connected, all of us here to summon our inner genies. I have no idea what to expect, but I know it will be fascinating. Over these nights, we're immersed in a swirl of ideas, manifestation practices, the language of the stars, whispers of the spirit world, and the solid backbone of plain old positive thinking. My notebook fills with messy scribbles; my mind swirling with possibility.

One session lodges itself deep inside me: the power of a vision board, I decide to make one. I start thinking what do I want to manifest for myself, what do I want my future to look like? I want to help people now that I'm sober. I want to write a book about my journey, an honest, stripped-back account of how I got sober and the mistakes I made along the way. I want it to be simple, clear, something anyone struggling could hold in their hands and think, *I'm not alone.* I see myself standing on a stage, sharing my story, my voice carrying into a sea of faces. I see myself traveling the world, inspiring people wherever I go.

I search online for images that match these visions. I print them, trim the edges, and glue them onto a board, arranging them like a map to the life I'm calling in. It hangs before me like a promise, a collage of dreams waiting to unfold.

And as you can see, right now, it works.

Late December, another opportunity presents itself: a 10-week program called *Accelerate Achievers*. with an energetic coach - known as - The Inspirational Medium. It's a deep dive into finding your "why," your life's treasure. It's exactly what I've now been searching for. I apply, get accepted, and join eleven others from across Australia. I manifested this, I know it!

We commence our first online session on 09th January 2024, we will meet each week and our coach will facilitate the two to three hour sessions, slowly peeling back the layers of our stories. We explore the shadows of our past, unearth the fears and beliefs that have been holding us back, and learn to dismantle them piece by piece. In this space, we're safe. We're honest. We're allies in each other's breakthroughs. And as we dig deeper, I can feel something inside me shifting, an unshakable clarity about where I'm heading next.

In one of the sessions, it happens, my breakthrough. It hits me like a bolt of lightning: *I am here to save people.* The words leave my mouth, and I feel chills rush over my skin. My whole body tingles with the truth of it. On the video call, the other participants can see the shift in me. It's as if someone has thrown open the curtains in a dark room. We all know this is a ground-breaking moment, not just for me, but for what I'm meant to do.

I finally have my *why*. I'm going to help people like me, people struggling with alcohol addiction to find the strength to quit, to live a better life, to know what I wasn't told. I want to give them the tools, the knowledge, and the encouragement to make recovery not just possible but sustainable. I want to guide them through the roughest parts, to be the steady voice I once wished I had. Just like I had envisioned when I created my vision board!

But now that I know my purpose, the question becomes—*how?*

Ideas begin spilling onto paper, workshops, talks, support groups and writing my story in full. I think about blending my love of connection with the tools and insights I've collected like precious stones along this journey. It's not just about sobriety; it's about living a life that feels full, intentional, and free.

This vision feels alive in my chest, like a spark that's been quietly waiting for me to notice it. And now that I have, I can't ignore it. My time in Tasmania isn't just about a fresh start, it's about planting something that can grow far beyond me.

Even with over forty years of lived experience, I want to be sure I have as much knowledge as possible to talk with authority and offer guidance rooted in more than my own journey. I decide to formalise my knowledge. I research courses and find a reputable institute offering a Certificate IV in Alcohol and Other Drugs (AOD). The moment I read the description, I know, it's the perfect next step.

I enrol and arrange to start in March. The course runs for twelve months, delivered online, with weekly live sessions led by a teacher and self-paced assignments in between. The curriculum is thorough, covering the science of addiction, the psychology of recovery, and practical ways to support people through the process. This is the foundation I need to step confidently into my new role. My plan is thoroughly in motion, now to let the universe do its magic.

I make it a point to fly back to Brisbane every two or three months to see my family. I miss them deeply, but I know I need to be in the right headspace before I even think about returning for good.

That turning point comes in March 2024. I fly up to Brisbane for a week to help my daughter-in-law with a campaign she's running. It is the most time we've ever spent alone together since I've known her, real, uninterrupted, one-on-one time. We talk, laugh, and share moments that deepen our bond.

Every evening that week, I'm with my son and also my two grandchildren. We play, we cuddle, we tell stories. And in those simple, ordinary moments, I realise something that hits me right in the heart, I'm missing their formative years. They're growing so quickly, and the love they have for me is pure and uncomplicated. Another seed is planted: I want to come back.

Originally, I'd promised myself I would stay for two years in Tasmania, I always knew it wouldn't be forever. Now, just eleven months in, the decision is already knocking on my heart. I talk to my son and daughter-in-law about the idea, and their reaction seals it, they're thrilled. They want me home. I'm over the moon. Decision made.

I return to Tasmania with a new sense of purpose: to close this chapter and prepare for the next. Brisbane is calling me back, and once again luck sits at my side. The company I work for owns multiple businesses under its umbrella, and as I scroll through the internal careers page, a role in Brisbane catches my eye. It seems written for me, perfectly aligned with my mix of skills. I apply, heart pounding with quiet confidence, and the offer comes through. Even better, it's an internal transfer. All I need to do is hand in my notice for my current role with an end date and set a start date for the new one.

Out of nowhere, in April, *his* emails return, slipping into my spam folder. Oh great, here we go again, I thought this was over. He writes that he *misses my company, he is lonely.* What the fuck! I shoot back a short reply, reminding him not to contact me, citing the protection order.

His response? Nasty. Then another, sharper. And another. Soon my inbox is poisoned with them, one after the other, acidic words piling up.

Once again, I find myself walking into a local police station to file a report. By the time I finish the paperwork, there are twelve breaches. By the time I'm back in Brisbane, the count has climbed to thirty-five I have reported.

And as I write these words now, the courts are still untangling the wreckage he insists on creating.

Until mid-July I'm still committed to house and pet-sitting in my little beachside community, so I sketch out the logistics: pack up, cross the strait, drive north, and begin my new role close to the end of July.

Once again, I load my car with my worldly possessions, every box, bag, and the hundreds of shells I have collected from the beaches, pieces of the life I've built. Stella and I roll onto the Spirit of Tasmania, the ferry's steel decks rumbling beneath, and we sail across the restless waters of the Bass Strait. The salty air stings my cheeks, and I watch the horizon darken and glow again, carrying me back toward the mainland. From Melbourne, the highway stretches ahead like a ribbon unfurling, guiding me home.

When I finally cross into Queensland, I can't stop smiling. I've done it. I uprooted myself, took risks, found my purpose, and now

I'm back where I belong, surrounded by family, standing firmly in the calling I've been handed. This isn't just returning home; it's returning home on a mission.

For the moment, I'm living with my bestie and her daughter, back in the very same complex I left just fourteen short months ago. To give us all a little breathing space, I line up a few house-pet sitting gigs around Brisbane. One of them, as it turns out, changes everything about my future living arrangements. The home is a stunning place in Kangaroo Point, tucked directly beneath the iconic Story Bridge, where the city lights spill across the river each night.

And then there are the dogs, two irresistible souls who steal my heart the moment I meet them. Dorothy, a stocky British Bulldog, and Columba, a mischievous little bull terrier with a streak of charm, are pure delight. Their personalities, adorable, cheeky, and downright hilarious,make every day with them a joy. Their owners are just as special, and almost immediately we strike up a friendship that feels as though it's meant to last.

Racing also calls me back. My first event is a sprint day at Morgan Park Raceway near Warwick. Engines roar, tires bite into the track, and the air carries the heady scent of hot rubber and fuel. We go out in groups of four, and as I grip the wheel, the circuit begins to flow under me. Lap by lap, my confidence grows until I let loose, adrenaline flooding my veins. By the end of the day, I've nailed fast, clean runs and times I'm proud of.

The season rolls on: two more Khanacross events, the Mount Cotton Hill Climb, and another sprint day at Lakeside Park Raceway. That last one brings me more than exhilaration, it earns me another award with the Club. I win my class for the RX Automotive Sprint Series and, at the BMW gala dinner, stand proudly as the plaque is placed in my hands. Another achievement. Another reminder of how far I've come.

Another milestone arrives this year: on August 31, I celebrate two years sober. At the Wynnum NA meeting, I sit among my peers with gratitude swelling in my chest. Beside me is one of my biggest supporters, the lovely woman I first met on the very night I walked through those doors. She has become not only an inspiration but a true friend, steady and kind, always reminding me of the strength I carry inside. I don't attend as many meetings these days, but I stay connected to the people who lifted me up when I needed it most, both in NA and AA. Their encouragement is stitched into the fabric of my journey.

As 2025 dawns, I choose to retire from racing. I've done what I set out to do. Back in 2023, I scribbled in my journal that I wanted a podium finish, and I achieved it. That chapter is complete. My focus now shifts to something deeper, something more lasting. My dream is to help others walking a path like mine, to tell my story with raw brutal honesty and courage, and this book is where that mission begins.

With the new year comes fresh change. I also retire from house-pet-sitting, with one exception: Dorothy and Columba. Those two charismatic bulldogs have claimed me forever, and I'm happily their Auntie Jane for life. I still stay with them now and then, curling up with their cheeky, snuffling and snoring companionship.

And now, finally, I step into a home of my own. I loved Kangaroo Point so much during that house sit that I've planted myself here for a while. The river glitters beneath the Story Bridge, the buzz of the city just beyond. My work changes too. The role I transferred into wasn't the right fit after all. But true to form, I land on my feet once again. An even better opportunity has opened up, perfectly aligned with my profession, and I embrace it as part of this new season of my life.

In the months that follow, I make a few trips back to Tasmania. Mum decides to sell her cottage and move into a retirement village, so I fly down in April to help her pack and again in May to unpack.

May holds something else for me too: the right time, finally, to start writing a book.

I have no idea where to begin. My journals stretch back to my very first rehab in May 2014, and reading them feels like wading through a tidal wave of memory. Overwhelmed, I turn to google, searching for how to write a book. The guidance gives me a skeleton, an outline, and with that, I start typing. Much of it is a messy brain dump, pages scattered and chaotic, but it's a beginning.

I send out inquiries, searching for help to shape the story. At the same time, I join a global mastermind group online, a gathering of people daring to build something of their own: businesses, courses, books. One post catches my eye, a man celebrating the publication of his book. I congratulate him and ask who his publisher is. His reply leads me to exactly where I need to be. The connection becomes the best decision I have made. I find the mentor who will guide me in bringing my story to life.

Today

August 31, 2025 I am three years sober. To celebrate, I publish this book. To show you that while there may never be a cure for alcoholism, there *is* a way forward. Don't just focus on the alcohol, dig deeper and find your why.

There is recovery.

There is hope.

With love,

Jane

Jane loves hearing from readers. Use the QR code or the link below to connect with her. Also, reviews are the heart beat of books. If you enjoyed this story, consider leaving a review wherever you purchased the book!

https://linktr.ee/MissJanesDiary

www.ingramcontent.com/pod-product-compliance
Lightning Source LLC
Chambersburg PA
CBHW052203090526
44583CB00015BA/1260